Surprised by Canon Law

Surprised by Canon Law
150 Questions Laypeople Ask about Canon Law

Pete Vere, J.C.L., and Michael Trueman, J.C.L.

PUBLISHED BY ST. ANTHONY MESSENGER PRESS
CINCINNATI, OHIO

Nihil Obstat: Reverend Robert J. McClory, J.C.L., J.D.

Imprimatur: Adam Cardinal Maida
              Archbishop of Detroit
              August 15, 2004

The *nihil obstat* and *imprimatur* are a declaration that a book is considered to be free from doctinal or moral error. It is not implied that those who have granted the *nihil obstat* and *imprimatur* agree with the contents, opinions or statements expressed.

Cover design by Steve Eames
Book design by Mark Sullivan

Library of Congress Cataloging-in-Publication Data

Vere, Pete.
   Surprised by canon law : 150 questions laypeople ask about canon law /
by Pete Vere and Michael Trueman.
      p. cm.
   Includes bibliographical references and index.
   ISBN 0-86716-608-8 (alk. paper)
      1. Canon law—Miscellanea. 2. Canon law—Popular works.   I. Trueman,
Michael, 1970- . II. Title.
   KBU160.V47 2006
   262.9--dc22

                         2004015667

ISBN 0-86716-608-8

Servant Books is an imprint of St. Anthony Messenger Press.
Published by St. Anthony Messenger Press.
www.AmericanCatholic.org
Printed in the United States of America.

Table of Contents

FOREWORD *by Patrick Madrid* vii

INTRODUCTION 1

CHAPTER 1: Introductory Questions and General Norms 3

CHAPTER 2: The Canonical Rights and Obligations of Christ's Faithful 11

CHAPTER 3: The Canonical Rights and Obligations of Clergy 21

CHAPTER 4: Structure and the Universal Church 29

CHAPTER 5: The Bishop and Diocesan Structure 33

CHAPTER 6: Priests and the Parish Structure 41

CHAPTER 7: General Questions on the Church's Teaching Office 47

CHAPTER 8: Catholic Schools and Universities 55

CHAPTER 9: Baptism 63

CHAPTER 10: The Sacrament of Confirmation 71

CHAPTER 11: The Celebration of the Holy Eucharist 79

CHAPTER 12: Reception of Holy Communion 91

CHAPTER 13: Confession and Anointing of the Sick 105

CHAPTER 14: Marriage and Annulment 113

HAVE ADDITIONAL QUESTIONS? 121

Index 123

FOREWORD

Michael Trueman and Pete Vere have prepared a very useful and timely resource in *Surprised by Canon Law*. Its title suggests how it is likely to be received by a popular Catholic audience—laypeople, religious, deacons, and priests. Many will be surprised by how simple and straightforward canon law really is.

For centuries, canon law has been for most Catholics a mysterious and esoteric aspect of Catholicism, a dimension of Church life that seems not just remote but inaccessible for the common man or woman. Not anymore. Now, with this book, Catholics in the pew will be able to not only "demystify" canon law but also gain a much clearer understanding of what canon law is and does (as well as what it does not do) and how it has been developed to help us along our common path toward heaven.

Far from being irrelevant to Catholics in the pew, canon law should be seen as a wonderful resource that informs us of our rights and obligations in the Mystical Body of Christ. The better we understand these things, the more effectively we can contribute to the health and well-being of the Church. Understanding canon law better will enable us to better promote harmony and unity.

Like any organization, the Catholic Church is governed by a set of well-thought-out, prudent laws that provide stability, security, and consistency to everyone involved. Just as no society could exist without laws, so too the Catholic Church. It needs canon law the way a freeway needs lane stripes. If there were no lane stripes, one can imagine the chaos and pandemonium that would reign on the highways! Canon law helps us maintain an orderly, just, and efficient running of the Church. And it goes without saying that the more clearly Catholics understand the "rules of the road," the better off everyone will be.

St. Paul provided us with an insight into the need for order and harmony in the body:

For by one Spirit we were all baptized into one body—Jews or Greeks, slaves or free—and all were made to drink of one Spirit. For the body does not consist of one member but of many. If the foot should say, "Because I am not a hand, I do not belong to the body," that would not make it any less a part of the body. And if the ear should say, "Because I am not an eye, I do not belong to the body," that would not make it any less a part of the body. If the whole body were an eye, where would be the hearing? If the whole body were an ear, where would be the sense of smell? But as it is, God arranged the organs in the body, each one of them, as he chose. If all were a single organ, where would the body be? As it is, there are many parts, yet one body. The eye cannot say to the hand, "I have no need of you," nor again the head to the feet, "I have no need of you."

—1 CORINTHIANS 12:13-21

In *Surprised by Canon Law*, the authors explain in a simple but effective manner the often obscure ways in which each member of the Church, whether lay, religious, or clergy, needs and depends on one another and how so many things in the life of the Church—the Holy Eucharist, the celebration of the sacraments, parish life, marriage and annulments, indeed a vast array of issues—are governed and guided by canon law. Some readers may be surprised to learn that canon law contains the answers to many questions that vex them:

"Why are non-Catholics not permitted to receive Holy Communion at Mass? Isn't that mean-spirited and divisive?"

"Can I attend the wedding of a Catholic relative who's marrying a non-Christian?"

"When is it appropriate for me to receive the sacrament of the anointing of the sick?"

"Is an annulment really just a form of 'Catholic divorce'?"

"When is an annulment a realistic possibility?"

"Will my children be illegitimate if my marriage is annulled?"

"Do Catholic parents have an obligation to send their children to Catholic schools?"

"May a layperson give the homily at Mass?"

These and other important questions are on the minds of many Catholics and even non-Catholics these days. This handy little book you're now holding will guide you through these questions, showing you not just the answers but the *reasons* for the answers.

— *Patrick Madrid*

Patrick Madrid is the author of ten books, including Search and Rescue *and* Where Is That in the Bible? *and the editor and coauthor of the acclaimed* Surprised by Truth *series.*

INTRODUCTION

Since the closing of the Second Vatican Council, many lay Catholics have begun to rediscover the riches of the sacred sciences. Whether it be through Dr. Scott Hahn's tapes on Sacred Scripture, a Patrick Madrid Catholic apologetics seminar, or a catechetical course at Catholic Distance University, Catholics are pursuing their faith with renewed vigor.

Yet what about canon law? To many Catholics—including pastors—this sacred science remains shrouded in mystery. It need not be so. Canon law is probably the most practical of sacred sciences; it is also among the most fascinating. It can be likened to engineering in that it deals with many of the nuts-and-bolts issues that theology only references in passing. In many instances canon law determines how theological truths apply to the daily practice of the Catholic faith. The Catholic layperson has nothing to fear from canon law. It is one of the many treasures God has given to help us achieve holiness.

The present authors can attest to this. Both of us are married laymen with families. We are licensed by the Church to practice canon law and have made practical careers serving Christ's faithful through the Church's ministry of canon law. We often field questions concerning canonical jurisprudence from fellow Catholic laymen, and we both derive a unique pleasure from answering these questions.

This work, then, represents a collection of the most common questions—well, 150 of them—that we have encountered within our various ministerial capacities. And we answer all of them! But the reader should not mistake this book for an exhaustive commentary on the *Code of Canon Law.* Nor is it intended to resolve disputed questions among experienced canonists. It is rather a starting point for understanding this backdrop of Church life.

So relax and enjoy this excursion into the sacred science of canon law. You might want to read just a question or two at a time. Or you might prefer to savor a chapter in the evening along with a warm glass of brandy, the nightcap of choice for most canon lawyers.

Regardless of how you read this book, it is our hope that you will learn something new *and* enjoy yourself in the process.

St. Raymond de Peñafort, patron of canonists, pray for us!

Pete and Michael
Pentecost
May 30, 2004

CHAPTER 1

Introductory Questions and General Norms

1. What is canon law and why is it important?

Every organization, whether secular or religious, requires its own laws and customs in order to maintain order. Within the Catholic Church, the internal legal system that governs its day-to-day workings is known as canon law.

Since the closing of the Second Vatican Council, Catholic laity have increasingly become aware of the science of canon law. Whether because of the rise in annulments or because of the crisis over sexual misconduct among the clergy, coming across references to canon law is no longer uncommon for most Catholic laity.

The word *canon* comes from the old Greek word *kanon*, which means "reed." In the ancient world, a reed symbolized the authority to rule. Thus the word *canon* means "to rule" or "the rule of law."

Now, returning to the original Latin, one finds two words for law—*lex* and *ius*. *Lex* refers to an individual or particular law. From its plural form *leges* we derive the English words *legislator* and *legislation*. The term *ius*, on the other hand, means an entire system of law or the subject of law in the abstract. From it we derive the English words *justice* and *jurisprudence*. When the Church employs the term *canon law*, she is referring to this *ius*. Thus the *Code of Canon Law* is known in Latin as the *Codex Iuris Canonici*.

2. What is a canon lawyer?

With the Church's internal legal system comes the need for professionals trained to function within this system. This is where canon lawyers, also known as canonists, come in. Typically, a canonist is one who has graduated from a program of studies at a pontifical faculty of canon law. Most canonists hold the licentiate (J.C.L.) degree. Some, after further study, obtain doctorates in canon law (J.C.D.) or in both canon law and civil law (J.U.D.). A few canonists have no degree in canon law but receive special permission from the Holy See to practice. Canonists may be clergy, religious, or laity.

Some canonists find work in a diocesan chancery office, where they assist the bishop in the administration of the diocese. Preparing a dispensation to permit a Catholic to marry a non-Catholic and drafting the constitutions of a new lay organization are just a couple of the ways a chancery canonist assists a bishop in diocesan governance. Other canonists end up teaching in Catholic colleges or schools, and a few even enjoy moonlighting as Catholic journalists.

Most canonists, however, find employment within the Church's tribunal system—that is, its court system. Within the tribunal, these canon lawyers function much like their secular counterparts. It may be as an advocate for a party, as a judge, as a defender of the bond in marriage cases (where the canonist defends the validity of the bond of marriage), or as a promoter of justice. This last office loosely corresponds to the position of district attorney or crown attorney within the secular justice system.

3. Why does the Church have a *Code of Canon Law*?

We need only think of the Ten Commandments as an example of how God has given law to his people. The new covenant of Christ gave birth to a new set of laws for the Christian community. The Church eventually used aspects of the legal system of the Roman Empire to enforce these laws. The Church, in turn, was the principal means of stability for Europe through the Dark Ages. Law kept the Church focused on its mission to evangelize the nations and provided an environment in which the Church was more receptive to God's plan.

The *Code of Canon Law* provides an orderly presentation of law. "Canons" are individual paragraphs of set law that the Church interprets and applies to given situations. Though the Roman Catholic Church has had collections of laws for many centuries, the *Code of Canon Law* was issued first in 1917, was revised in 1983, and will more than likely be revised in the future as the Church faces new challenges. The Eastern Catholic Churches have their own code of law, which was issued in 1990.

The Church does not need a **Code** *of Canon Law*, but it has chosen to use such a structure. Canon law deals with the day-to-day affairs of the Church.

4. Does the *Code of Canon Law* contain all the laws of the Church?

There are different types of law in the Church. The most important law is divine law, or law that has been revealed through Scripture. For example, the eighth commandment mandates that people not bear false witness.

Another type of law is ecclesiastical law, or laws made by the pope and the bishops of the Church. Ecclesiastical laws fall into many different categories: liturgical law (that is, how to worship), sacramental law (how to celebrate the sacraments), ecumenical law (how we work with other Christians), and so on.

The *Code of Canon Law* cannot contain all the laws of the Church. As canon 2 explains, "For the most part the Code does not determine the rites to be observed in the celebration of liturgical actions." Each diocese and religious order has its own particular laws, which are not included in the Code.

Though you will not find all the laws of the Church in the *Code of Canon Law*, it is certainly a good starting point. It includes seven unique divisions, called books:

Book I, *General Norms*, lays down the ground rules of the Church's legal system.

Book II, *The People of God*, looks at who makes up the Church.

Book III, *The Teaching Function of the Church*, tells how we proclaim the gospel of Christ through teaching.

Book IV, *The Sanctifying Function of the Church*, deals with our sanctification by Christ in the sacraments.

Book V, *Temporal Goods*, gives guidance on how we are to deal with worldly goods.

Book VI, *Penal Law*, describes the Church's responses to errant behaviors.

Book VII, *Procedural Law*, explains legal processes in the Church.

5. Does the *Code of Canon Law* apply to all Catholics? Does it affect non-Catholics at all?

The *Code of Canon Law*, or *Codex iuris canonici* by its proper Latin title, was issued for the Latin Catholic Church (the Roman Catholic Church). Therefore, it applies to all Latin Catholics.

There are a number of Catholics in the world who are not Latin Catholics. The Latin Catholic Church developed in Rome, Western Europe, and the Americas, but the Catholic Church also exists in Eastern Europe, the Middle East, Africa, and other parts of the world as what is commonly called the Eastern Catholic Churches. In the same way that Latin Catholics are unique, there are twenty-one distinct Eastern Catholic Churches. These twenty-one Catholic Churches were given their own code of law in 1990, and the Latin Church's *Code of Canon Law* does not apply to them.

The *Code of Canon Law* can place obligations on non-Catholics. Whenever divine law is cited in the *Code of Canon Law*, non-Catholics must oblige. For instance, a Protestant person who was divorced would need a declaration of nullity of his or her first marriage (an annulment) from the Catholic Church in order to marry a Catholic (see Question 148).

The *Code of Canon Law* also extends privileges to non-Catholics. For example, canon 1183, paragraph 3, permits a funeral in the Catholic Church for a baptized non-Catholic whose own minister is not available.

6. What are general norms?

As previously mentioned, the *Code of Canon Law* is divided into seven books. *General Norms*, the first book, contains the general principles that guide canon lawyers in interpreting the code. Strictly speaking, general norms are the general rules and principles of law invoked by canonists when interpreting the various legal texts promulgated by the Church.

Canon 9 is an excellent example of a general norm. This canon states, "Laws concern matters of the future, not those of the past, unless provision is made in them for the latter by name." As a general principle, this means laws should never be retroactive; it is unfair to bind someone to a law that does not yet exist. Thus, should a situation arise in which the good of the Church requires that a law be retroactive, then the law itself must specifically provide for its retroactive force.

In a broader sense, *General Norms* also includes a number of key definitions of canonical terms. These canonical terms are found throughout the Code, as well as throughout various other legal texts. Canonists use these definitions to discern more clearly the meaning behind certain canons. For example, canon 23 defines *custom* as a practice "introduced by a community of the faithful." (See Question 10 for more about customs.)

7. What is the difference between the terms valid and licit in canon law?

Validity concerns the substance of the act, whereas the word *licit* refers to its lawfulness. For example, back in 1988 Archbishop Lefebvre consecrated four bishops without first obtaining a papal mandate from Pope John Paul II. This act was valid because Archbishop Lefebvre is a validly consecrated bishop and so has the faculty to consecrate other bishops. But the archbishop not only failed to observe the canonical prohibition against consecrating bishops without the Holy Father's permission, he actually proceeded with the consecrations after the Holy See directly ordered him not to do so. As a result of this unlawful action, the Church excommunicated Archbishop Lefebvre and the four bishops he had consecrated illicitly.

Nevertheless, the bishops consecrated by Archbishop Lefebvre for his Society of St. Pius X (SSPX) are real bishops. They have the power to administer the sacraments just as does any Catholic bishop. The Church does not reconfirm any individual who leaves Archbishop Lefebvre's schism to return to the Catholic Church. The Church also recognizes the priesthood of any SSPX priest who approaches the Holy See and requests to be reconciled with the Catholic Church.

The situation differs with Anglican or Episcopalian laity and clergy who wish to be received into the Catholic Church. The Catholic Church does not recognize the validity of Anglican orders—that is, the Church does not believe Anglican holy orders can be traced back to the Apostles in an unbroken fashion. Therefore, the Church requires that the sacrament of confirmation be repeated whenever an Anglican or Episcopalian is received into full communion with the Catholic Church. And a man who has received Anglican orders must be ordained in the Catholic Church if he wishes to function as a Catholic priest.

8. How do we know if an individual canon is speaking of lawfulness or validity?

While there are some exceptions to the following, canons 10 and 39 generally outline when a condition within an individual canon affects the validity of an action. Canon 10 states, "Only those laws are to be considered invalidating or incapacitating which expressly prescribe that an act is null or that a person is incapable." In other words, the individual canon must specify that "for validity" a certain condition must be met for an action to take place, or that "one is incapable" of fulfilling a certain action.

The first paragraph of canon 900 presents an excellent example of how this canonical principle works: "The only minister who, in the person of Christ, can bring into being the sacrament of the Eucharist is a validly ordained priest." In keeping with the canonical principle of canon 10, if someone other than a validly ordained priest attempts the consecration at Mass, transubstantiation does not take place. The bread and wine remain bread and wine.

When an action is administrative, canon 39 offers additional criteria for distinguishing between what concerns validity and what concerns lawfulness only: "Conditions attached to an administrative act are considered to concern validity only when they are expressed by the particles 'if,' 'unless,' 'provided that.'" An example of an administrative act is a dispensation allowing a Catholic to marry an unbaptized person. For validity, this dispensation requires the approval of the local ordinary or his delegate (see canon 1086).

9. Must canonists always be strict in their interpretation of individual canons?

An old Roman legal principle states that favors are to be multiplied and burdens restricted. Therefore, a law bestowing a favor upon a particular group or individual should be interpreted to apply in as many situations as possible. On the other hand, a law that restricts the canonical rights of a group or individual, or otherwise imposes a burden, should be interpreted narrowly.

This principle is reflected in canon 18 of the current *Code of Canon Law*. "Laws which prescribe a penalty, or restrict the free exercise of rights, or contain an exception to the law, are to be interpreted strictly," the canon states. Canon lawyers understand a strict interpretation to mean one restricted in its application to as few cases as necessary. This restrictive interpretation applies in three types of situations: (1) those involving penalties for violating canon law; (2) those involving the restriction of one's canonical rights; and (3) those involving an exception to canon law.

For example, canon 1398 automatically imposes the penalty of excommunication upon a Catholic who procures an abortion. However, canon 1323 states that nobody is subject to a canonical penalty who "has not completed the sixteenth year of age." Because excommunication is a penalty and must be restrictively interpreted, a fifteen-year-old who is pressured into aborting her child does not incur the automatic excommunication under canon 1398. Nevertheless, the act of aborting her child in the womb remains objectively sinful.

10. What is a custom in canon law?

A custom is a practice that arises within a community of Christ's faithful. In contrast, legislation is imposed from above by the Roman pontiff or the diocesan bishop. The community must be "capable of receiving a law," which means that the Holy Father or the diocesan bishop could impose a law similar to the custom upon the community if needed. An example of a custom in many parishes is the holding of hands during the recitation of the Our Father at Mass.

According to canon 24, a custom must be reasonable. For instance, a custom that would prove divisive to the community is not reasonable. Similarly, a custom can never be contrary to God's law. Therefore, the Church could never tolerate a custom that permitted adultery, abortion, the worship of false gods, or any other practice that is contrary to divine law or natural law.

In keeping with canon 27, "custom is the best interpreter of laws." Should a custom continue uninterrupted for thirty years, or should the competent legislator (namely, the Holy Father or the diocesan bishop) approve the custom, then the custom takes on the force of law within the community.

CHAPTER 2

The Canonical Rights and Obligations of Christ's Faithful

11. Who makes up the Church, and how do we understand the Catholic Church in relation to other Christian communities?

Canon law sometimes makes theological statements, and canon 204 is one such example. The first paragraph of this canon identifies "Christ's faithful" as "those who, since they are incorporated into Christ through baptism, are...the people of God." Baptism is the sacrament that makes one a Christian.

Christ's Church is comprised of *all* the world's baptized people. Nevertheless, as Catholics, we hold that Christ's Church has its full expression in the Catholic Church (canon 204, paragraph 2). This has been maintained through the unbroken communion shared among Catholic bishops, with the successor of Peter, the pope, at its head (canon 336).

Christians take no pride in the fact that Christ's Church is divided, and indeed they should not. Christ's vision is "that all may be one" (Jn 17:23), and Catholics must work toward the restoration of unity. Bishops have a special obligation in this regard (canon 383, paragraph 3). Ecumenical work, though directed by the bishops, is the responsibility of all Catholics.

Christ's faithful in other Christian churches and communions witness the work of grace. As Catholics, we cannot overlook heresy or theological error, but we can seek to better understand and highlight the aspects of faith that we share. The starting point is baptism.

12. What does being in communion mean in respect to the Eastern Catholic Churches, the Orthodox Church, and Protestant denominations?

Being in communion means "belonging to the Catholic family." Canon law specifies what is needed for communion:

baptism (canon 204)
profession of faith (canon 205)
celebration of the sacraments (canon 205)
acknowledgment of ecclesiastical governance (canon 205)

A profession of faith is best articulated in the Nicene Creed, which we recite at Mass, or the Apostles' Creed. Acknowledgement of seven sacraments, especially the real presence of Christ in the Eucharist, is necessary for maintaining communion. Ecclesiastical governance, or recognition of the authority of the college of bishops and the primacy of Peter's ministry in the person of the pope, is the final facet.

We are therefore left with varying degrees of communion with other Christians. Full communion is best expressed within the Catholic Church, of course. Full communion exists between Latin Catholics and Eastern Catholics.

With the Orthodox Church we share baptism, profession of faith, and the sacraments. The Orthodox Church does not recognize the ministry of the pope in the same way that it is understood in the Catholic Church.

With Protestant denominations we share baptism and possibly profession of faith. Very few accept and celebrate seven sacraments. Protestant denominations do not acknowledge any papal influence in their church structure.

An Orthodox or Protestant person can enter communion with the Catholic family. On the other hand, if a Catholic were to reject the profession of faith, the validity of the sacraments, or Christ's mandate to the bishops to govern the Church, he or she would break communion with the Church.

13. What does it take to become a Catholic?

The Latin phrase *Semel catholicus, semper catholicus* means "once a Catholic, always a Catholic." One becomes Catholic by baptism in the Catholic Church or by a public profession of faith in the Catholic Church. Determining who is and who is not Catholic is important in canon law, since the law ordinarily does not extend rights to or place obligations on non-Catholics (see the exceptions cited in Questions 5 and 148).

Canon law clearly upholds the practice of infant baptism: "Parents are obliged to see that their infants are baptized within the first few weeks" (canon 867, paragraph 1). Baptized Catholic infants remain Catholic for the rest of their lives. If a baptized Catholic denounces God or joins another religion, he remains a Catholic though he is not in full communion with the Church.

When a baptized non-Catholic (for example, a Protestant) wants to become Catholic, the Catholic Church usually recognizes the baptism of the individual and requires only a public profession of faith. This is preceded by a course of religious instruction, usually provided through the Rite of Christian Initiation of Adults (RCIA). The sacraments of confirmation and Holy Communion follow. If this individual has a baptized child over the age of seven who also wishes to become Catholic, the child is also expected to make a public profession of faith with his or her parent or parents. These people also never cease being Catholic.

14. I am Ukrainian Orthodox, but since my wife is a Roman Catholic, I would like to be a Roman Catholic too. How do I become one?

First you must make a profession of faith, and then you must apply for a transfer into the Roman Catholic Church. The profession of faith acknowledges the ministry of the pope, in union with the world's Catholic bishops. Once a person makes this profession of faith, he or she becomes a member of the closest corresponding Eastern Catholic Church. In your case, you would become a Ukrainian Catholic.

In order to then become a Roman Catholic, you must ask for a transfer of churches. You can do this by writing to the Vatican; however, the more common means is by asking your Ukrainian Catholic bishop to release you from the Ukrainian Catholic Church. You must also receive the acceptance of a Roman Catholic bishop. In fact, permission to leave an Eastern Catholic Church will not be granted without the previously arranged acceptance into the Roman Catholic Church.

Gaining permission to transfer from an Eastern Catholic Church to the Roman Catholic Church is not easy, and one needs a good reason to do so. It so happens that in the case of a marriage such as yours, such permission is usually given in order to promote unity within the family.

15. Do I have a right to tell my pastor or bishop what my parish or diocese needs?

The simple answer is "Of course you do." Church law clearly states that the baptized "have the right,...in keeping with their knowledge, competence and position, to manifest to the sacred Pastors their views on matters which concern the good of the Church" (canon 212, paragraph 3). In fact, it is the responsibility of every Catholic to do so.

This law is to be taken seriously, since the Church not only witnesses to the spiritual reality of our lives but also exists and ministers within the world and has to deal with all sorts of earthly matters on a day-to-day basis. We must share with pastors our insights and ideas regarding how the Church might better conduct its affairs. We rely on one another for good judgment. In turn, Church law obliges the pastors of the Church to consult the laity on many important decisions.

This right and duty is not to be regarded as an ongoing brainstorming session, and prudence must be exercised in this regard. Raising concerns is best done in "keeping with [one's]...competence and position." The canon ends with the reminder that everyone must "show due reverence to the Pastors and take into account both the common good and the dignity of individuals."

16. Do Catholics have a right to the sacraments?

The sacraments are the ways that the faithful are sanctified and brought deeper into the life of Christ. It is well stated in the *Catechism of the Catholic Church* that the sacraments "give birth and increase, healing and mission to the Christian's life of faith" (CCC 1210).

The law ensures that the sacraments are available to the people of God. It states, "Christ's faithful have the right to be assisted by their Pastors from the spiritual riches of the Church, especially by the Word of God and the sacraments" (canon 213). More importantly, the law goes on to say, "Sacred ministers may not deny the sacraments to those who opportunely ask for them, are properly disposed and are not prohibited by law from receiving them" (canon 843, paragraph 1).

#2
Ryft

This canon points out that access to the sacraments is not absolute: A person has to be "properly disposed" to receive them. For instance, an engaged couple who does not have adequate insight into the nature of marriage is required to postpone marriage until they understand the seriousness of the vocation.

Furthermore, a parish is only obliged to supply the sacraments to its own parishioners. For example, a priest may offer marriage to a couple who are not parishioners, but he is not bound to do so.

17. What is the "right of association" for Catholics, and to what does it extend?

As human nature would have it, we are apt to find like-minded people and join with them to promote some value or activity that we hold to be of benefit. When we come together in this way, we form an association.

Canon law encourages and protects a right to establish and belong to associations. Canon 215 explains, "Christ's faithful may freely establish and direct associations which serve charitable or pious purposes or which foster the Christian vocation in the world." In some parts of the world this is a profound statement. The gospel of Christ must be proclaimed, and baptized people enjoy a sacred right to fulfill their vocation in the world.

 # 3
Ryft

The law notes three fundamental reasons for Christians to establish associations: to conduct charitable works, to promote piety, and

③ to foster the Christian vocation. The right of association expects Catholics, both laity and ordained, to work together, in dynamic ways, to proclaim the gospel.

Canon law goes one step further. Canon 298 explains that Catholics can establish associations *within the Church* that are distinct from religious orders. These associations can be officially recognized and given a status in law to promote Christian teaching, public worship, evangelization, works of piety and charity, and bringing the Christian faith to the secular world. Nevertheless, if an association within the Church intends to offer Christian teaching in the name of the Church, encourage public worship, or do what is proper to the ministry of the Church (for example, provide parish missions), the association must gain a mandate from a Church authority, such as a bishop.

18. What relationship does a Catholic association have with the larger Church?

Bishops throughout the world direct the Catholic Church. Gathered together with the pope, these bishops are assisted by priests, deacons, and the laity to carry out Christ's mission. All members of Christ's faithful must expend a concerted effort to advance the well-being of the Church.

Catholic associations, whether they be closely or remotely associated with the ministry of the Church, must assist the bishops in promoting the message of salvation. As we discussed in Question 17, Catholics have the right of association, but these associations are created to advance the work of the Church. ① ②

There are two types of Catholic associations: private and public. Their main difference is that the assets of a private association belong to the individuals, whereas the assets of a public association are at the immediate use of the Church. An example of a private association is the St. Joseph Foundation. An example of public associations can be found in the recent Roman approval of certain movements in the Church, such as the Cursillo Movement and the

Charismatic Renewal. A competent Church authority, such as a diocesan bishop, approves the establishment of both types of associations. These groups are invariably born out of some grass roots effort to better express the Christian life. The Church officially recognizes associations because of the enduring value of their work in light of the gospel. Associations can be given legal personality and then enjoy certain rights in canon law; however, associations also have obligations to the Church. The law gives greater autonomy and places fewer expectations on private associations than on public ones.

19. What does Church law have to say about protecting the reputations of others?

Canon 220 states, "No one may unlawfully harm the good reputation which a person enjoys, or violate the right to protect his or her privacy."

Every person enjoys the right to a good reputation. This is a natural law written into the human conscience. Any person of good will knows not to frustrate the reputation of another. We need only think of Christ's teaching to be wary of criticizing others (see Lk 6:41-42).

There are cases in which individuals need to be reprimanded publicly, even though such actions might harm their reputations. Consider, for example, a group of parishioners who reject a teaching of the Church. It would be inappropriate for the pastor, on first knowledge of such error, to publicly harm the group's reputation. He must attempt to understand the group's position and give the members an opportunity to correct their position. But if these parishioners persist in their rejection of the truth and their promulgation of the error after being warned, the pastor's obligation is to publicly point out their waywardness, perhaps through a letter to the parish.

Another means of publicly challenging a person's reputation is through a penal trial. For instance, a priest guilty of sexual abuse of a minor can be dismissed from the clerical state. The priest's reputation is certainly shattered. Nevertheless, no member of the Church can threaten the reputation of this priest until the penal trial is concluded.

20. What obligations does the laity have to support the Church?

Christ promised that he would not abandon his Church; however, its temporal existence and the fulfillment of its mission in the world require the assistance of all Christ's faithful. Canon 222 states that Christ's faithful have the obligation to support the Church, "so that the Church has available to it those things which are necessary for divine worship, for works of the apostolate and of charity." The second part of this canon calls for a promotion of social justice "to help the poor" and for the worthy support of the ministers who carry out the work of the Church.

Christ's faithful must have churches that inspire our praise of God in the celebration of the Divine Liturgy (that is, the Mass). Thus a bishop's initiative to build a new church ought to receive favorable financial support. Artisans, architects, contractors, financial advisors, cleaners, and so forth all provide their talents.

Diocesan and papal charities require enormous support from the laity, not only financially but through the work of many hands. Christ provides the model of a preference for the poor; Catholics should be living examples of his love for the needy. This includes directly assisting them out of our own resources.

21. As a layperson, do I have a right to be an extraordinary minister of Communion?

Laypeople do not enjoy a "canonical right" to be extraordinary ministers of Holy Communion, and laypersons who are appointed to the role may be restricted as to when the role can be exercised. Let me explain.

The emergence of extraordinary ministers of Holy Communion was caused by a need. A sizable number of Catholics gather for Mass, and the assistance of laypeople was needed for distribution of

Holy Communion. Laypeople can be appointed in a stable and permanent manner to this sacred role (canon 230, paragraph 3). There is a reason why the word *extraordinary* is used when referring to those who perform this task. The *ordinary* ministers of Holy Communion are bishops, priests, and deacons. In 1987 the Vatican was asked for a clarification on the function of extraordinary ministers of Holy Communion. The Vatican replied that when ordinary ministers are present in the church, even if they are not participating in a formal way at Mass, they must distribute Holy Communion. This might mean that an extraordinary minister is not needed at a particular celebration.

One further note: Though it is not explicitly mentioned in the law, if a person's life is at odds with Christian moral teaching, it is inappropriate for him or her to be appointed or, if already appointed, continue in this sacred function.

22. Are the canonical rights of Christ's faithful absolute? Or does the *Code of Canon Law* subject one's canonical rights to certain limitations?

Besides the limitations already noted, canon 223 provides Catholics with some general boundaries when it comes to exercising one's canonical rights. The first paragraph of this canon states:

obligation

> In exercising their rights, Christ's faithful, both individually and in associations, must take account of the common good of the Church, as well as the rights of others and their own duties to others.

In short, no canonical right is absolute. Rather, canonical rights are to be understood in the context of one's obligations toward the whole Church. Thus one must always exercise one's canonical rights in view of the common good, meaning the good of both the Church as a whole and the good of one's particular Church community. The canonical rights of the individual can never supercede those of the Church or those of others.

The second paragraph of this canon continues, "Ecclesiastical authority is entitled to regulate, in view of the common good, the exercise of rights which are proper to Christ's faithful." In order to preserve the rights of all Catholics, limitations must sometimes be placed upon the exercise of the canonical rights of a particular individual. When such a need arises, the Church's lawfully appointed pastors have both the right and the obligation to impose the limitations.

Chapter 3

The Canonical Rights and Obligations of Clergy

23. Who is primarily responsible to promote vocations to the priesthood and religious life?

The whole of the Christian community has a duty to nurture vocations to the priesthood and religious life. In the current climate of a sizeable reduction in the numbers of active clergy, people realize the benefit, even the urgency, of promoting vocations. Canon law explains that the responsibility falls to "Christian families, educators and, in a special way, priests, especially parish priests" (canon 233, paragraph 1).

The canon places the largest responsibility for vocation promotion on diocesan bishops. It is they who must "show the greatest concern...and instruct the people entrusted to them on the importance of the sacred ministry."

24. Who is responsible for the establishment and running of seminaries?

There are two types of seminaries: those founded and operated by dioceses and those founded and operated by religious orders. A diocesan seminary typically trains deacons and priests for ministry within the diocese, while an order seminary trains men for ministry or religious life within its own community.

It is the primary responsibility of the diocesan bishop to promote vocations within his diocese. If a bishop deems it useful, he is to establish a minor seminary in which college-aged men are given religious formation as they acquire "human and scientific [academic] education" (canon 234, paragraph 1).

Canon 233, paragraph 2, recognizes that people of mature age—perhaps a widower whose children are grown—may be interested in being ordained. Protestant ministers who become Catholic sometimes receive permission from the Vatican to be ordained, since the law of mandatory celibacy is an ecclesiastical law for the priesthood (that is, not God's command) and can be relaxed in such cases.

In preparation for ordination, all candidates for the priesthood "are to receive the appropriate religious formation and instruction...in a major seminary" (canon 235, paragraph 1). If possible, each diocese is to have a major seminary (canon 237, paragraph 1). This is not financially possible in many dioceses, so interdiocesan seminaries have been founded. Permission to form interdiocesan seminaries must come from the Vatican.

A diocesan bishop is the only one who may admit a candidate for the diocesan priesthood to a major seminary. If a man wants to begin studies in a diocesan seminary, he needs to be nominated by a bishop. It is also the diocesan bishop, on the recommendation of the seminary staff, who will approve the candidate for ordination.

25. What is a permanent deacon, and who can become one?

Having fallen into disuse sometime during the Middle Ages, permanent deacons were reintroduced after the Second Vatican Council. In the 1917 *Code of Canon Law* there were only "transitional" deacons, or deacons on the path of ordination to the priesthood.

Permanent deacons must take part in a three-year preparation period. They may be "young men" (twenty-five to thirty-five years of age) or "more mature men" (thirty-five and older). The young men must be celibate, but "more mature men" may be married (canon 236). The law also adds that married men must have the consent of their wives before being ordained.

Permanent deacons who have a secular career are to use their own resources to support themselves and their family; those who work full-time for the Church "deserve" to be sufficiently compensated (canon 281, paragraph 3). This canon is significant in that the entire diocese takes on a certain level of responsibility for a permanent deacon upon ordination. The law does not require that the permanent deacon be employed full-time, since there are some dioceses and parishes that cannot compensate adequately for such work.

The day-to-day role of the permanent deacon is not outlined in canon law. Unlike other ordained clergy, they do not have to wear clerical attire, are not restricted from holding public office in civil government, may manage money and engage in commerce or trade, and may take an active role in political parties and unions.

26. Can priests move from diocese to diocese, assignment to assignment?

The law does not permit "freelance" priests. "Wandering clergy are by no means to be allowed" (canon 265). A priest must formally belong to some structure, whether it be a diocese, a personal prelature like Opus Dei, or a religious order like the Franciscans. Belonging to one of these groups is called incardination. If you ever should question the authenticity of someone's claim to be a priest, you can always ask him where he is incardinated.

Most Catholics are accustomed to priests who spend their lives serving parishes in a particular diocese. There are also priests who belong to religious orders. They live with other priests of the order and perform ministries in keeping with the mission of the order. For example, the Franciscans have a ministry to the poor, so a priest of this order might serve the homeless. From time to time religious order priests will serve in diocesan parishes on the invitation of a bishop.

Though rare, a diocesan priest may be permitted by his bishop to perform ministry outside of a parish setting, even in another part of the world. This is usually done for a specified period of time, and the diocese to which the priest goes must be willing to care for his needs. If the priest spends a number of years ministering in such a place, he can ask to be incardinated into that diocese or into a religious order with which he is serving.

Within a diocese or religious order, any priest can and does receive new assignments. Experience has shown us that this is healthy. It supplies priests and parish communities with new personalities and opportunities for spiritual growth.

Obligation *Ob*

27. Our pastor has been preaching the same thing for years. Is he required to update his studies?

Priests are obliged to continue their sacred studies (canon 279, paragraph 1); to attend pastoral courses, theological meetings, or conferences (paragraph 2); and to seek knowledge in the secular sciences (paragraph 3). Though the tenets of the Catholic faith remain constant, we can deepen our understanding of the faith. This requires prayer and study. It is not unreasonable to expect this of our pastors.

It is unfortunate when priests preach about the same things, year after year. From one perspective, the truth of the Christian gospel does not change, and a homily is not strictly a teaching moment. It is a time to enliven the faith of those gathered so that they may be better disposed for the reception of Holy Communion. It is a moment of proclamation. Nevertheless, the faithful need to hear this unchanging truth in new and vibrant ways.

The gospel is not preached in a vacuum. Pastors should preach in light of the issues that pervade our lives. Therefore, the homily should be a time to reflect on contemporary issues that the Church and the human community are facing. This presumes that the preacher is knowledgeable about such issues.

Evangelization requires pastors to consider those to whom they are preaching. Thus some knowledge of the secular sciences is also beneficial for the priestly ministry, as it helps develop a dialogue and rapport with a highly technical, scientifically minded Western society.

28. We've seen our pastor become more and more caught up in fashion and nice cars. Can he do this?

Obligation

Canon law clearly says, "Clerics are to follow a simple way of life and avoid anything that smacks of worldliness" (canon 282, paragraph 1); "clerics are to shun completely everything that is unbecoming to their state" (canon 285, paragraph 1); and "avoid whatever is foreign to their state" (paragraph 2). They are forbidden to assume political office (paragraph 3) and may not manage goods belonging to laypeople (paragraph 4).

It is fair to say that Christians in many countries of the Western hemisphere do not mirror the simplicity of life Christ proclaimed. Our religious leaders are caught between the same two poles as the rest of the population: gospel simplicity and affluent materialism. Does this mean that a priest is not to drive a car, take a holiday, or read a best-seller? No. This canon simply reminds clerics to rely on Christ and his Church for their well-being.

If a bishop, priest, or deacon receives what is over and above what he needs, he "may well wish to use [it] for the good of the Church and for charitable works" (canon 282, paragraph 2). One way to help hold fast to simplicity of life is to minister directly to "the poor, the suffering, the lonely, those who are exiled from their homeland, and those burdened with special difficulties" (canon 529, paragraph 1).

29. Our pastor has inherited a small business, and it seems to me he is more interested in running the business than providing for the parish. Can he do this?

Diocesan priests do not make a vow of poverty, so they can acquire material goods (see Question 27). Yet bishops, priests, and some deacons may not practice commerce or trade, even for the benefit of another, without the permission of ecclesiastical authority (canon 286). In the *Code of Canon Law* from 1917, if a priest violated this norm, he would receive an automatic penalty.

Your pastor must have received permission to run his father's business; however, it is likely that the permission was issued for a determined period of time. The reason for your concern is the reason for the canon: Clerics should not be distracted in their ministry. Furthermore, bishops, priests, and deacons are in positions of influence, and it must not appear that they use that influence in the business setting.

The canon does not prohibit the management of a clerics' own assets. A bishop, priest, or deacon can put his money in the stock market or other sorts of investments. It should also be noted that permanent deacons are exempt from the provisions of this canon.

30. At a recent political convention, our pastor was elected to a leadership role within the party. This bothers people in our parish. Should he be doing this?

In the past the Catholic Church has strongly influenced political movements. The Church's social teaching also has supported the rights of workers to form unions, and clerics have been at the forefront of these politically charged labor movements. Nevertheless, canon law prohibits bishops, priests, and some deacons from assuming an "active role in political parties or in directing trade unions" (canon 287, paragraph 2).

There are two exceptions to this prohibition. If the Church's welfare is at stake, permission can be given for the bishop, priest, or deacon to play an active role in a party that supports the Church's rights. For example, in a country where Christianity is suppressed, a priest could be allowed to take on a leadership role in a political party that is attempting to change the unjust laws.

The second exception occurs when there is a benefit to the common good of a given population. For instance, a priest could be given permission to help direct a political party that is pro-life in its purpose.

In closing it can be said that such tasks are not the responsibility of the spiritual leaders of the Church. It would be better for clerics to advise lay politicians and labor leaders to use their own time, talents, and energy in this way. (Also see Question 56.)

31. Can the Church take the priesthood away from a priest?

The short answer is: Once a priest, always a priest. Like baptism, once a person is ordained, despite any heinous acts he may commit later in life, the effect of his ordination remains for life.

There is one exception to this rule. If it can be shown that there was something fundamentally wrong at the time of the ordination, then a declaration can be made that the so-called priest was not validly ordained. For example, a man forced against his will to accept ordination is not validly ordained.

Though a validly ordained priest does not ever cease being a priest, he can be removed from the clerical state. This means that he may no longer function as a priest or enjoy any support from the diocese or religious order to which he belonged. Canon 290 permits the removal of the clerical state in one of three ways:

- The priest or his bishop can ask the pope for "laicization."
- A three-judge panel within a diocese can try a priest's actions. The judges review evidence, allow the priest to present his case, and make a decision. Not all crimes in canon law warrant dismissal from the clerical state.
- An office in the Vatican may remove a priest from the clerical state through a simple decree if circumstances warrant.

CHAPTER 4

Structure and the Universal Church

32. Does use of the title Catholic require any authorization?

As with any reputable institution, the Church safeguards the title *Catholic* in order to ensure that Christians know that a group using this title has the written endorsement of a Catholic Church authority. This authority is usually the bishop of the diocese.

The Church has no way to enforce this law; however, in practical terms, if one is suspicious of the authenticity of a group that claims to be Catholic, one can simply request to see such written permission. For instance, there are a number of fringe Marian groups that do not enjoy favor with the Church. Some of these groups solicit funds from Catholic individuals. In some cases, well-meaning pastors will allow the groups' advertising materials to be on display in the foyers of their churches.

A school must have the approval of an appropriate authority (for example, the bishop) to bear the title *Catholic.* The law states, "No school, even if it is in fact catholic, may bear the title 'catholic school' except by consent of the competent ecclesiastical authority" (canon 803, paragraph 3).

33. Why do we have a pope, and what is the scope of his authority?

As one might expect, canon law has a number of things to say about the pope. In law he is usually referred to as the Roman Pontiff, a title that was influenced by the title of emperors in the Roman Empire. The role of the pope, however, has theological origin.

Peter received Christ's mandate to build his Church. Peter ministered in the ancient city of Rome and eventually died there, so Rome is regarded as the diocese in which Peter's successor continues his ministry. Canon 331 explains, "The office uniquely committed by the Lord to Peter, the first of the apostles, and to be transmitted to his successors, abides in the Bishop of the Church of Rome." The canon goes on to say that the pope is the "head of the college of bishops," and as head he must maintain and promote the restoration of Christian unity throughout the world.

The pope has immediate authority not only over the diocese of Rome but also over the universal Church. "By virtue of his office, he has supreme, full, immediate, and universal power in the Church, and he can always freely exercise this power." His vigilance over the universal Church gives him the authority to make laws for the Church. It was by the hand of Pope John Paul II that the 1983 *Code of Canon Law* was created for every diocese and religious community throughout the world.

34. Can the pope resign?

We are witnessing something extraordinary in modern times. His Holiness John Paul II is the most traveled pope in history, and given the length of his term in office, he has likely met more people than any other before him. As well, unlike other popes, the world has watched him struggle with his health. This has given rise to the question, Can he resign?

Though traditionally the pope remains in office until death, he can certainly resign. Canon 332, paragraph 2 states:

> Should it happen that the Roman Pontiff resigns from his office, it is required for validity that the resignation be freely made and properly manifested, but it is not necessary that it be accepted by anyone.

Since the pope has "supreme, full, immediate, and universal power in the Church" (canon 331), his actions are not dependent upon another's response. Thus his resignation does not need to be accepted.

How then could a pope resign? A pope would have to clearly state his resignation in spoken word or in writing. He also could make provision in writing that if he were to become completely incapacitated in his judgment, his resignation would be automatic.

Nevertheless, this exists merely in the realm of possibility; no such law actually requires the pope to make such a provision.

35. To what age are priests, bishops, and cardinals expected to work?

Priests who still hold the office of pastor are expected to submit a letter of resignation to their bishop once they've turned seventy-five (canon 538, paragraph 3), but they are not obliged to do so. If a priest has the wherewithal to continue in ministry, he may. Most priests in developed countries belong to pension plan programs, and by the time they reach their seventy-fifth year, they are ready to retire. Interestingly, U.S. bishops may permit their priests to retire at an earlier age, but since there is a shortage of active clergy, we may see more and more priests of retirement age continuing to work full-time.

A bishop who has turned seventy-five "is requested to offer his resignation from office" to the pope (canon 401, paragraph 1). A retired bishop assumes the title "bishop *emeritus*." *Emeritus* is simply the Latin word for retired.

Cardinals who head offices in the Vatican are "requested to offer their resignation from office" for the pope's consideration when they reach the age of seventy-five (canon 354). The cardinals have concern about another age. In a document called *Universi Dominici Gregis* (1996), Pope John Paul II continued the tradition that once cardinals complete their eightieth year, they no longer enjoy voting privileges in the election of a new pope.

Since theirs is a vocation, priests, bishops, and cardinals do not usually stop celebrating the sacraments and performing other acts of ministry after their retirement, just as married couples do not cease being married upon retirement.

36. What sort of gathering was the Second Vatican Council? Does the law have anything to say about when we will have another?

The authority to teach the Catholic faith lies in what we call the *magisterium*. Sacred Tradition and Sacred Scripture make up a single sacred deposit of the faith (CCC #97); however, it belongs to the apostles and their successors to transmit and teach the faith from one generation to the next.

An ecumenical council is a gathering of the world's Catholic bishops to discuss and teach the Catholic faith. Such meetings are ancient in origin.

It is the prerogative of the pope to call an ecumenical council. As the successor of Peter, the first among apostles, he presides over the affairs of the council (canon 338, paragraph 1). He can suspend the council, end it, and approve its conclusions. He sets the agenda and approves items added to the agenda by other bishops. His authority is so considerable that if he does not approve the decrees of the ecumenical council, they have no effect on the Church. This, of course, has not been the practice of the popes.

Vatican II (1962-65) was an ecumenical (meaning "worldwide") council and an occasion for the *magisterium* of the Church to be manifested in "solemn form" (canon 337). It came at a time when the Church was facing a world of immense change. There is no way to tell when the Holy Spirit will prompt a pope to call for another ecumenical council.

Chapter 5

The Bishop and Diocesan Structure

37. Why are there dioceses, and what is the function of diocesan bishops?

The word *diocese* derives from a Greek word whose earliest meaning refers to managing a house. As time went on, it came to refer to administering or governing a certain area. Every Catholic in the world belongs to a diocese (or an equivalent structure), and every Catholic has a bishop (or an equivalent) and a pastor (or an equivalent).

Church law places much emphasis on territorial boundaries, since Catholics exercise their rights and fulfill their obligations in the territories in which they live. This territorial structure ensures that Catholics all over the world have a church to which they belong.

Bishops usually oversee dioceses. Priests, deacons, and the laity assist a bishop in the day-to-day function of parishes within a diocese. Canon 375 explains that bishops, as successors of the apostles, are "to be the teachers of doctrine, the priests of sacred worship and the ministers of governance." Though priests fulfill these same purposes, they are regarded as collaborators in the mandate given to their bishop. They defer to their bishop on matters of teaching, sanctifying, and governance.

The bishop maintains communion with the rest of the world's Catholic bishops. If a bishop breaks this unity, the law strips him of any authority over his diocese (canon 375, paragraph 2). An example of this occurs when a bishop attempts to ordain another bishop without permission from the pope. The result is *latae sententiae* (that is, automatic) excommunication.

38. Why do some bishops hold the title of cardinal, and what is their function?

An individual becomes a cardinal only through appointment by the pope. The world's cardinals form what is called the College of Cardinals. These individuals are given the function of cardinal because of their significant and noteworthy contributions to the Church. They are esteemed as extraordinary Church leaders.

The College of Cardinals is an entity that is not found in Scripture but was created by the tradition of the Church. Its primary function is very simple: to elect a pope.

The laws concerning the election of a pope are not contained in the *Code of Canon Law* but in a document that was issued by Pope John Paul II in 1996 called *Universi Dominici Gregis*. The document explains that at any given time the pope is to ensure that there are no more than 120 cardinals under the age of eighty who are available to elect the successor of Peter. Sometimes the number of voting cardinals drops below 120. There is no significance to this number other than that it represents a sizeable sample of the world's Catholic leaders who will discern who will be the next pope.

Canon law acknowledges another function of cardinals. They must also be available to the Roman Pontiff, either acting collegially, when they are summoned together to deal with questions of major importance, or acting individually, that is, in the offices which they hold in assisting the Roman Pontiff especially in the daily care of the universal Church (canon 349).

39. Is it not enough to have one bishop in a diocese? Why are there auxiliary bishops?

One bishop is all that is needed in order for a diocese to function as outlined in canon law. However, a diocese might have a large Catholic population and a large number of parishes. Though assisted by priests, deacons, and the laity, the diocesan bishop can find it difficult to meet the pastoral needs of his diocese. In this case he may request the assistance of an auxiliary bishop.

A diocesan bishop can submit the name of a potential auxiliary bishop to the pope. If the pope gives his papal mandate (approval), the consecration can take place.

An auxiliary bishop enjoys all the theological and spiritual significance of a bishop and is regarded as a member of the world's College of Bishops; however, he does not have the authority to manage the diocese in his own name, and he may not establish diocesan law. Furthermore, he is not the next in line to take over leadership of the diocese. The law requires that the auxiliary bishop assist the diocesan bishop in carrying out the diocesan bishop's direction for the diocese, and not his own (see canon 407, paragraph 3).

Canon law requires the diocesan bishop to give auxiliary bishops the power to fully exercise the administrative role of a bishop, which among other things means he can relax certain laws and make decisions binding on Catholics in the diocese. This assumes the diocesan bishop has not reserved a specific situation or case to himself.

40. Who runs a diocese when there is no bishop?

There comes a time in the life of every diocese when its diocesan bishop resigns, dies, or is transferred to another diocese. Replacing a bishop takes time, since suitable nominations must be presented to the pope and a number of individuals must be considered for the responsibility. In the meantime, a diocese needs to continue its day-to-day affairs. The law has a mechanism to help in this transition.

When a diocese is without a diocesan bishop, the Apostolic See (that is, the Vatican) is notified of the vacancy. It should be noted that the Apostolic See may intervene and impose an apostolic administrator on the diocese. But normally the selection of the administrator is handled by a diocesan organization, the College of Consultors. This group of priests, previously appointed by the diocesan bishop, meets within eight days of the vacancy and elects a diocesan administrator. The name of the diocesan administrator is then forwarded to the Apostolic See.

The appointed administrator acts as a caretaker of the diocese while it waits for a new bishop. He manages the diocese with all the administrative authority of a bishop. The diocesan administrator is to make no innovation in the way the diocese is run or make a decision that would inhibit the freedom of the eventual incoming bishop. A diocesan administrator who is not an auxiliary bishop does not enjoy the sanctifying power of a bishop. For instance, the diocesan administrator cannot consecrate the sacred oil of chrism that is needed for the sacrament of confirmation.

41. Does an archbishop have authority over other bishops in his area?

A bit of history is helpful here. After missionaries brought the faith to a country, including the Americas, dioceses were established. As the Church grew in numbers within a particular area, new dioceses were carved out of the enormous area of land that once made up the founding diocese. Thus a relationship began. The founding diocese was regarded as the metropolitan diocese, and the smaller dioceses were known as the suffragan dioceses.

The law maintains this distinction. The bishop of the metropolitan diocese or archdiocese assumes the title of archbishop or metropolitan archbishop. Since the original diocese oversaw the establishment of the smaller dioceses, the archbishop is regarded as the one who must ensure that the Church is doing well in his diocese and the suffragan dioceses of his ecclesiastical province. Canon law explains that he is "to see that faith and ecclesiastical discipline are carefully observed and to notify the Roman Pontiff if there be any abuses." He may conduct official visits of suffragan dioceses, with the permission of the pope, if certain matters appear to be neglected there (canon 436).

People may express concern to the metropolitan archbishop about how their own diocese is functioning. Though the metropolitan archbishop has no authority other than vigilance, he can determine whether or not the matter ought to be brought to the attention of the Vatican. However, a good principle of law is that the first place to express concern is to your own bishop.

42. What is the function of the Conference of Catholic Bishops in my country?

In each country (or region of the world), Catholic bishops join together in an association called a conference of bishops. This is an expression of the cooperation that bishops share in a country or region. As successors of the apostles, the bishops are a visible sign of unity in proclaiming the gospel of Christ. The conference provides them with the opportunity to combine insights in order to better relate the gospel to the unique challenges that face their particular part of the world. This body takes on a prophetic character when it articulates the teachings of the Church.

Some conferences of bishops are very well organized and can heavily influence the affairs of the Church in their particular country. Nevertheless, the purpose of a conference of bishops is to assist individual bishops in their ministry. Each bishop retains full authority over his diocese. The pope and his offices in the Vatican deal directly with an individual bishop, and a conference of bishops is not regarded as an intermediary body. As a rule, a conference of bishops does not possess the authority to force individual bishops and their dioceses to follow decisions made by the conference.

In some instances—for example, setting the minimum age for confirmation (see canon 811)—canon law allows a conference of bishops to determine just how a law will take expression in a country or region. For instance, the Canadian Conference of Catholic Bishops has agreed that the assignment term for a pastor is either six years, renewable, or indefinite. This is binding on all bishops in Canada.

43. How can my bishop gather information and make decisions on important issues facing the diocese?

There are a number of committees that need to be set up by a diocesan bishop. Each diocese must have a council of priests (canon 495) and a college of consultors (canon 502). It is highly advisable for a bishop to also establish a diocesan pastoral council (canon 511), comprised of priests, deacons, members of religious communities, and laypeople who represent a sample of the population of the diocese. A bishop must visit each parish of his diocese, either personally or through a delegate, within a five-year period. These are ways that the bishop remains aware of the issues facing Catholics in the diocese.

Another, more significant mechanism in canon law, called a "diocesan synod," gathers people of the diocese around the bishop to discuss a certain theme or issue (canon 460). Diocesan synods have been used rarely in recent decades, but the law still upholds them as a valuable means of addressing the needs of a diocese.

After consulting the council of priests, it belongs to the diocesan bishop to decide that a diocesan synod would be beneficial. Member delegates at such meetings must represent all Catholics in the diocese. Canon 465 explains, "All questions proposed are to be subject to the free discussion of the members in the sessions of the synod." The members of the synod must vote on resolutions; however, it is up to the diocesan bishop to decide whether or not synod decisions are turned into law for the diocese.

44. Who manages the day-to-day administration of the diocese?

A bishop can be overwhelmed with the day-to-day operations of the diocese, and it is better to share this responsibility with another person than to attempt to do it all himself. The law insists that if the size of the diocese warrants it, at least "one Vicar general is to be appointed" (canon 475, paragraph 2) to attend to the administrative affairs (executive branch) of the diocese.

The executive branch of governance ensures that the law and discipline of the Church and diocese are followed. The vicar general can serve as an official representative of the diocese at certain functions with dignitaries and media. He may even be the one who hires and fires diocesan staff.

Given the nature of administration, the law strongly insists that a vicar general also be appointed as the moderator of the curia. *Curia* is the Latin word for "office." The moderator of the curia oversees diocesan staff and agencies that serve the well-being of parishes and parishioners in the diocese.

45. What is the role of the chancellor in my diocese?

Canon law requires each diocese to have a chancellor. The 1917 *Code of Canon Law* required a priest for this role, but the 1983 *Code* allows the appointment of a layman or laywoman to this office.

The chancellor is the principal notary of the diocese. He or she prepares written records of the affairs of the diocese and ensures that decisions affecting various individuals or the diocese as a whole are made known to the people affected by such decisions. It is a great advantage if the chancellor knows canon law, since he or she must draft the decrees (that is, the written decisions) made by various authorities within the diocese.

Depending on the diocese, a chancellor may be responsible for tasks that do not properly belong to the role. Canon law makes provision for this by acknowledging that "particular law" or local diocesan law may add responsibilities to the chancellor's primary task, which is "to ensure that the acts of the curia [that is, diocesan offices] are drawn up and dispatched, and that they are kept safe in the archive of the curia" (canon 482).

The chancellor must maintain the diocesan archives. There are three different types of archives in a diocese: a general archive (canon 486), a historical archive (canon 491, paragraph 2), and a secret or confidential archive (canon 489). The chancellor is responsible for the first two. Only the diocesan bishop manages the secret archive.

46. Who makes the business decisions in my diocese?

The mission of the Church is to proclaim the gospel and work toward the salvation of souls. The Church has acquired material goods to assist in these tasks. The assets of a diocese can grow quite large, and good business and financial decisions need to be made on a day-to-day basis.

Aware of the fact that not all bishops or vicar generals have the wherewithal to make solid financial decisions, the law requires that in each diocese a finance committee is to be established. "It is to be composed of at least three of Christ's faithful, expert in financial affairs and civil law, of outstanding integrity, and appointed by the Bishop" (canon 492).

The finance committee is responsible for preparing an annual budget and an annual financial report. On some matters, the diocesan bishop cannot go against the advice of the finance council.

A financial administrator must also be appointed in each diocese. "The financial administrator is to be expert in financial matters and of truly outstanding integrity" (canon 494, paragraph 1). The financial administrator must ensure that the annual budget is followed. He is also to make payments of diocesan funds that have been authorized by the bishop or his delegate. The financial administrator must make a report to the finance committee at the end of the fiscal year.

47. Do the priests in my diocese have a representative body? How do they make known their complaints?

The law requires that in each diocese the bishop must establish a council of priests (canon 495). This is a representative organization that is an accurate sample of priests in the diocese. Some members are elected, and some are appointed. The bishop is to use this body to help him understand the needs of his diocese.

Though the law emphasizes the advantage to the bishop, the council provides a venue in which the priests can articulate their concerns for the Church and help the bishop to make decisions that enhance the "pastoral welfare" of the people of God throughout the diocese. Priests are the backbone of the institutional Church. Though the bishop carries the mandate of the apostles, the priests are the ones who have immediate and personal contact with Christ's faithful in the parishes.

CHAPTER 6

Priests and the Parish Structure

48. Can I attend and be a member of any parish I like?

The quick answer is "Nobody is going to stop you!"

This is a topic for which law has not caught up with life. In the past, people attended the church within whose boundaries they resided. Now some people "church shop," looking for better music, a prettier worship space, or perhaps a priest who conducts the liturgy and preaches in a gratifying way. Some pastors even encourage people to register in a parish in which they do not reside.

However, canon law has something to say about this. Canon 518 explains that a parish is "to be territorial, that is, it is to embrace all Christ's faithful of a given territory." Thus the law provides a structure in which every Catholic belongs to the parish by virtue of residence. People have the right to insist on spiritual care from their territorial pastor, and a pastor cannot deny the sacraments to the parishioners of his parish.

Two problems have arisen with the "church shopping" phenomenon. First, some churches have lost the financial support they need. Secondly, some pastors deny marriage to people who are within their parish boundaries because they are not "registered," while providing marriage to those who are registered but live outside the territorial boundaries.

49. Must my parish have a pastor?

How things change! There was a time when parishes had two or three resident priests, and now dioceses in many countries are struggling to place a priest in each parish. With no sign of immediate change in most Western countries, the Church is doing what she can do to answer the needs of the faithful.

The bishop must provide pastoral care either personally or through the ministry of a pastor. Ordinarily a parish "is entrusted to a parish priest as its proper pastor" (canon 515). In the current struggle to staff parishes, bishops are reluctant to appoint priests to the role of pastor since they may need to move them later. Nevertheless, bishops must keep in mind that despite the anxiety created by the shortage, pastors enjoy a right to stability in their assignments.

It can happen that one priest is made pastor of many parishes. Though the law states that a priest is obliged to reside "in the parochial house near the church" (canon 533), this is not always possible. He may, therefore, live elsewhere, perhaps in a location central to his various responsibilities.

In the case of a sudden leave of absence, a parish administrator may be appointed to fulfill the pastor's role. A parish administrator functions in the same way as a pastor, but unlike a pastor, he does not enjoy stability in the assignment. In other words, he can be moved at the bishop's discretion. See Question 55 for more information on the parish administrator.

50. What can I expect of my pastor?

Canon 528, one of the longest canons in the *Code of Canon Law*, outlines the responsibilities of a pastor. Pastors have a twofold obligation: They must proclaim the gospel and work toward the salvation of souls.

The pastor is obliged to proclaim the Word of God to those living within the territory of his parish. Through his homilies and religious instruction, he must teach the faith to his parishioners, especially to children and young people. He must be attentive to issues of social justice and encourage his parishioners to become engaged in such matters. He has the unique responsibility of encouraging parishioners to join him in seeking out those who have lapsed in the practice of their faith. He must encourage those who do not profess the true faith to seek conversion.

The pastor must encourage Catholics to appreciate the spiritual heritage of the Church. He must ensure that the Eucharist is the focus of the parish. He must promote the regular reception of Holy Communion and the sacrament of penance. He must ensure that all the sacraments are celebrated in a devout, proper fashion and be vigilant in preventing abuses from creeping into the liturgy. He must persuade the laity to take an active part in the liturgy and to pray in their own homes.

51. Anything else?

Canon 529 outlines further obligations. In order to know the Catholics entrusted to his care, the pastor must visit "their families, sharing especially in their cares, anxieties, and sorrows, comforting them in the Lord." He is to "help the sick,…seek out the poor, the suffering, the lonely, those who are exiled from their homeland, and those burdened with special difficulties." He must work to support spouses and parents in their vocations and to promote Christian life in general.

The pastor is to recognize gifts in the laity that can promote the Church's mission. He is to foster associations of the faithful so that the work of the Church can be carried out more effectively. The pastor is to see to it that parishioners are concerned for the well-being of their parish.

The pastor also works with his bishop and other priests of the diocese to connect parishioners to the diocesan and universal expressions of the Church. He must encourage his parishioners to take part in diocesan and universal Church events.

As one can imagine, the tasks these canons envision would require the work of Christ himself. This canon is an inventory more than a checklist. These are the most important aspects of the pastor's ministry and form a sort of "pastor's manifesto."

And in return, the laity offers its support. "Christ's faithful…are bound to show Christian obedience to what the sacred Pastors, who represent Christ, declare as teachers of the faith and prescribe as rulers of the Church" (canon 212, paragraph 1).

52. It seems my pastor is away a lot. How much vacation is he allowed?

Canon law provides a one-month vacation each year to priests (canon 533, paragraph 2). Since law is a discipline of precision, it also defines one month as thirty days (canon 202). U.S. and Canadian dioceses provide one day of rest per week for priests, and it may be argued that these days are not normally counted among the thirty days of vacation. As in the secular workplace, a priest is not obliged to take his vacation all at one time. He can take a day or two, here and there. He can even combine a day of rest with a vacation day and take two days off per week for most of the year.

As well, every priest and deacon is required to make a spiritual retreat once a year (canon 276, paragraph 2, number 4). This retreat can be of varying length and is not regarded as vacation time (canon 533, paragraph 2).

Nobody monitors a priest's vacation time, and he is not obligated to report his used vacation days to the diocese. However, if a pastor is away from his parish for more than a week at a time, he must tell the diocesan bishop, the vicar general, or an auxiliary bishop of his absence so that arrangements can be made to supply another priest who will care for the parish in his absence.

53. It seems the parish council is running the parish. What authority does it have?

There is no way a parish council can run a parish. The management of a parish is given to a pastor (or parish administrator) and is well regulated in canon law. The parish council is only an advisory body that assists the pastor in fulfilling his obligations to a parish.

It is the prerogative of the diocesan bishop to establish parish councils in the parishes of his diocese if he "considers it opportune" (canon 536). If he regards them as valuable mechanisms of operation, each parish is required to have one. For those dioceses that have parish councils, guidelines should be issued. In the current climate of collaborative models of ministry, the faithful know their role in the Church and expect to provide input in areas in which they are specialized (for example, finances, construction, and so on).

The law is clear: The parish council is consultative in nature. Even if the members of a parish council were unanimous and adamant about a certain course of action for the parish, the pastor would not be obliged to follow their direction. Nevertheless, it would be folly for him not to heed the sound advice of such a group. He could expect an appeal to the bishop if a course of advised action were not taken.

54. I'm concerned about the parish finances. To whom does the pastor have to report?

Some parishes struggle to manage money, while others have larger operating budgets than most small businesses. Regardless, every parish must have a finance committee (canon 537).

Canon law establishes a parish as something called a "juridical person." Since money and property are important parts of the day-to-day function of the Church, in order to ensure a responsible management of money and property, the law states, "Every juridical person is to have its own finance committee…who are to assist in the performance of the administrator's duties" (canon 1280).

As we have seen in examining the parish, the pastor assumes this role of administrator. The pastor does not have to follow the finance committee's advice. But it would be imprudent of him not to heed such advice if the finance committee is comprised of financial experts from the parish—which it should be.

Canon law does not explain how a finance committee is structured; it leaves this determination to the local diocese. There is, however, a practice in canon law to look to other canons for direction. In this case the diocesan finance committee can serve as a model. It is composed of three members who are experts in financial and civil law.

55. My pastor was removed last year, and we have a parish administrator. What is his function, and how long can we expect him to be around?

The law mentions a few reasons for pastors' unplanned leaves: imprisonment, exile, banishment, and poor health among others (canon 539). Most of the time pastors leave because of health problems or scandalous behavior. The pastor may be away for an undetermined period of time, but unless he is formally removed as pastor, he retains his title. If he is able to return to his parish, he continues as pastor.

In the meantime, the bishop must supply a priest, if possible, to care for the needs of the parish. The person who takes the place of the pastor is called a parish administrator. He must be a priest who, once appointed, assumes all the responsibilities of a pastor (see Questions 50 and 51). He may not, however, make changes that compromise the work of the pastor after the pastor's return.

There appears to be an increase in the practice of bishops' assigning priests as parish administrators rather than pastors. This is a wrong application of the law. Pastors enjoy a right to stable ministry, and the role of parish administrator is transitory in nature. The appointment only lasts as long as the pastor is away or, if the pastor has been removed, until the next pastor is assigned. A batch of priest assignments occurs usually once a year in most dioceses.

CHAPTER 7

General Questions on the Church's Teaching Office

56. Why doesn't the Church butt out of the government's making of public policy?

The influence of the Church on government policy has fluctuated throughout the centuries. Political authority persecuted the early Church, while later the Holy Roman Empire was an arm of the Church in the political governance of Europe. Behind all these dynamics is the command of Christ to proclaim the gospel to all nations. The Church not only has an obligation to influence public affairs, it also claims a divine right to proclaim the gospel.

Canon 747 explains that the Church has the authority to proclaim the gospel "independent of any human authority." The Church is required to pass on, from one generation to the next, the essential teachings of the Christian faith. These essential teachings come from the revelation of God through Jesus Christ. We teach what Christ has taught us: what God desires of us and how we are to make our lives pleasing to him. Therefore,

> the Church has the right always and everywhere to proclaim moral principles...and to make judgments about any human matter in so far as this is required by fundamental human rights or the salvation of souls. (canon 747, paragraph 2)

It follows that as Christians we must influence government policy. Though our concern and focus is on the kingdom of God, Christians are not to retreat from the world around us. (Also see Question 30.)

57. Does the law clarify the notion of papal infallibility?

Many people struggle with this dogma. In order to understand it more fully, try reading some good Catholic theology. In particular, we would recommend the *Catechism of the Catholic Church*, Pope Pius XII's *Mystici Corporus,* and the Second Vatican Council's "Pastoral

Constitution on the Church" (*Gaudium et Spes*). That being said, canon law makes a few points that will help clarify infallibility of the pope.

The pope teaches in an infallible way when, by "definitive act," he teaches "a doctrine to be held concerning faith or morals" (canon 749, paragraph 1). In other words, not everything the pope teaches has the weight of infallibility. He must make it clear that the content of his teaching is being stated definitively. For instance, in 1954, when Pope Pius XII taught that Mary was assumed into heaven upon her death, he said, "We declare, pronounce, and define that it is a divinely revealed dogma that the immaculate mother of God . . . was assumed body and soul into heavenly glory."

The College of Bishops also has the ability to teach in an infallible way (canon 749, paragraph 2). When gathered in an ecumenical council, bishops may "definitively declare for the universal Church a doctrine to be held concerning faith and morals." Even outside an ecumenical council, if the bishops come to agree on a teaching, together with the pope, it can be definitively declared as infallible.

In order to avoid confusion on this issue, the law states, "No doctrine is understood to be infallibly defined unless this is manifestly demonstrated" (canon 749, paragraph 3).

58. What is heresy, and what are its consequences?

Heresy is "the obstinate denial or doubt) after baptism, of a truth which must be believed by divine and catholic faith" (canon 751). You will notice that the law does not associate heresy with wrong teaching but with not believing true teaching. Therefore, nonbaptized people cannot be heretics. Heresy usually involves a public pronouncement of a teaching that is contrary to an essential teaching of the Christian faith. It involves a baptized person who refuses to believe what is true, even after the truth has been explained to him or her.

A distinction needs to be made between heresy and theological error. We are human beings who struggle with understanding the divine. Laity and clerics alike make theological errors. A theological error can be corrected. If it is not, and if it concerns an essential Christian teaching that must be believed, it becomes heresy.

Heresy is subject to the penalty of excommunication. When a person knowingly teaches something contrary to the fundamental tenets of the Christian faith, that individual places himself or herself outside of communion with the Catholic Church. A Vatican office called the Congregation for the Doctrine of the Faith usually investigates claims of heresy.

59. Is there a penalty for joining another religion?

Apostasy

The offense of abandoning the Christian faith is called *apostasy*. Apostasy is the "total repudiation of the Christian faith" (canon 751). *Repudiation* may be defined as "a rejection or intentional denial." In order to be an apostate, an individual must be a baptized Christian (see Question 12 in Chapter 2).

Joining another religion does not necessarily constitute apostasy. Misguided people might find no conflict between Christianity and another religion to which they are attracted. In their minds, they continue to be Christians. This is not apostasy. Likewise, if a Catholic joins another Christian denomination, even with the intention of abandoning the Catholic faith, this is a sinful action but not apostasy.

Apostasy is a "total repudiation of the Christian faith" and results in instant excommunication. The act of apostasy itself causes the excommunication, and a Church authority does not need to get involved. In order to return to the Christian faith, the individual has to renounce the error, make a confession, and have the penalty of excommunication removed. In the meantime, the individual may not benefit from the ministry of the Church.

There is no penalty of excommunication when a Catholic joins another Christian church, as this is not apostasy. However, the effect is similar. The Catholic may not receive Holy Communion until he or she makes a formal return to the Church through confession and a profession of faith.

60. What is schism? How does schism differ from heresy and apostasy?

Canon 751 defines schism as "the withdrawal of submission to the Supreme Pontiff or from communion with the members of the Church subject to him." Unlike heresy, in which one obstinately denies a defined teaching of the Church, or apostasy, in which one completely repudiates the Christian faith, a schismatic neither rejects nor denies Church teaching. Rather, those in schism refuse to submit to the judgment of the Roman Pontiff.

A well-known schism is that of Archbishop Lefebvre and his followers. The Archbishop consecrated four bishops against the express wishes of Pope John Paul II. The Church subsequently declared Archbishop Lefebvre—as well as the four bishops he consecrated and the faithful who adhered to his actions—excommunicated for the crime of schism.

One can also become schismatic by refusing communion with the members of the Church subject to the Roman Pontiff. Suppose, for example, a priest refuses to recognize the authority of his diocesan bishop and founds a parish without the bishop's permission. Should such a priest persist in his refusal to submit his parish to the legitimate authority of the diocesan bishop, the Church may judge this priest and those within his parish guilty of schism.

In accordance with canon 1364, paragraph 1, the penalty for schism is automatic excommunication.

61. What is the required response of Catholics to teachings of the Church?

There are a number of ways to respond to Church teaching, depending on the weight of the teaching itself. Belief in the essential matters of faith (canon 750) is a requirement. Even if we do not logically understand a teaching (for example, the Incarnation or the Blessed Trinity), through belief we can know it is true. These are things that "must be believed." Without these items of faith, one is not regarded as a Catholic.

Another type of response is to acknowledge that a Church teaching is exact and truthful (canon 752). The Catholic then must act on such an understanding. For instance, harvesting embryos for stem cell research is wrong, and avoiding involvement in any such research is the expected response.

Some aspects of Catholic teaching require agreement and action. The Christian has to avoid sin. Otherwise, one may not regard oneself as Catholic or even Christian.

Another type of response is to acknowledge that Church teaching is accurate but does not require any action (canon 753). For instance, a conference of Catholic bishops may propose that a particular television program is offensive and harmful to Christians. A Catholic must publicly acknowledge this teaching; however, the individual may have his or her own conclusion.

Finally, all Catholics are obliged to respect the everyday decisions of their bishops and priests as they apply Church teaching locally.

62. Why have a diocesan bishop if the pope is the one we are to listen to?

Christ's mandate to Peter was to administer his Church in collaboration with the other apostles. The Church has come to understand that there are two expressions of the same Church: one at the local level and one on the universal level. Canon law states, "The office of preaching the Gospel to the universal Church has been committed principally to the Roman Pontiff and to the College of Bishops," and, "For the particular Churches...that office is exercised by the individual Bishops, who are the moderators of the entire ministry of the Word in their Churches" (canon 756).

The pope's authority comes through the mission that Peter received from Christ; however, this mission is exercised in communion with all the bishops of the world. It is inaccurate to think that the pope is a CEO and the bishops are branch managers. When it comes to preaching and teaching, they are to be regarded as peers, with the pope responsible for the universal Church and therein having special prerogatives.

The local Church has pressing needs that the pope is not aware of or has no time to attend to. These local needs are not his mandate. The bishop has the faculty to proclaim the gospel and minister to the Church in his area.

63. May a layperson give a homily?

A layperson may preach but may not give a homily.

Canon 766 explains that the "laity may be allowed to preach in a church or oratory if in certain circumstances it is necessary, or... advantageous." In some parts of the world, where there is a shortage of priests or deacons, the laity can be permitted to preach. For instance, in Canada's northern territories there may be no priest or deacon who can converse in the language of the people. When the faithful gather there for the Liturgy of the Word, with or without distribution of Communion, an assigned layperson may preach.

There are also occasions at Mass when the laity can offer insights. For instance, a finance committee member can address the congregation before Mass begins or after the final blessing.

Though a homily is a form of preaching, it is "reserved to a priest or deacon." By virtue of ordination, clerics (that is, bishops, priests, and deacons) have the responsibility to proclaim the gospel and give the homily. It is the moment in which the baptized are taught the mysteries of faith by the pastors of the Church.

Mass on Sundays and holy days of obligation must include a homily; only for a grave reason may it be omitted (canon 767, paragraph 2). The law also strongly recommends that there be a homily at weekday Mass (canon 767, paragraph 3).

64. Is my pastor primarily responsible for teaching the Catholic faith to my family and me?

The responsibility to teach the Christian faith belongs to all the baptized; however, canon law identifies a number of people who have special duties in this regard.

Parents and godparents. Canon 774, paragraph 2, explains that before all others, "parents are bound to form their children, by word and example, in faith and in Christian living." Catholic godparents also assume this responsibility. The special responsibility of parents is not satisfied merely by sending their children to a Catholic school.

The bishop. The diocesan bishop is responsible for preparing standards for catechetical instruction (religious instruction). He also must ensure that resources are available in the diocese and prepare, if necessary or possible, a "catechism," which is a textbook or handbook concerning aspects of our faith (canon 775, paragraph 1). The bishop must also make sure that efforts are made to advance catechetical instruction in his diocese.

The pastor. The pastor must "ensure the catechetical formation of adults, young people and children" (canon 776). Along with other clerics and religious sisters and brothers, he is to make himself available for religious instruction. These people must not "refuse to give their labors willingly." Finally, the pastor must remind parents of and assist them in their responsibility to form their children in the faith and Christian living.

Chapter 8

Catholic Schools and Universities

65. What is the Church's role in Catholic education?

Parents have the obligation and the right to educate their children (canon 793, paragraph 1). They must send their children to schools that will provide Catholic education (canon 798). If children are not sent to Catholic schools, parents are to provide Catholic education outside the school. In some dioceses where there are no Catholic schools, parishes provide Catholic education in a limited fashion; however, the responsibility still rests with parents.

Like parents, the Church not only has the obligation but also claims the right to provide Catholic education (canon 794). Pastors have the duty to make Catholic education available to all the faithful. The Church has the "right to establish and to direct schools for any fields of study or of any kind and grade" (canon 800, paragraph 1).

Nothing requires science and religion to be taught separately. Catholic teaching on faith and morals cannot remain indifferent to contemporary issues of our nation and our world. Catholic education attempts to impart knowledge within the context of faith. It is a unique method of instruction for grade school, high school, and post-secondary institutions.

66. Our pastor rarely visits our grade school. Does he have an obligation to do so?

There is nothing in the *Code of Canon Law* that explicitly requires a pastor to visit a school associated with his parish; however, many canons of the *Code* certainly imply this.

Canon 777 explains that the pastor must make sure that "adequate catechesis is given for the celebration of the sacraments" and that children are properly prepared for first confession, first Holy Communion, and confirmation. Even after children are given their first Communion, the law calls on the pastor to give "a richer and deeper catechetical formation." The Catholic school often provides this catechesis, so it seems necessary for the pastor to frequently visit the school in order to support and enhance the religious education the teachers there are imparting.

It is the right of the diocesan bishop to "watch over and inspect the Catholic schools" (canon 806, paragraph 1). The bishop may also issue "directives concerning the general regulation of the Catholic schools." He must also make sure that the Catholic school is "in its academic standards, at least as distinguished as...other schools in the region" (canon 806, paragraph 2).

67. There are no Catholic schools in our diocese. Who is responsible to establish such schools?

The Catholic Church must be commended on initiatives it has taken to educate people. Though its early schools were established primarily as means of religious instruction, there are many parts of the world that would have gone without a school system had it not been for the Church. Nevertheless, there are parts of the world that still do not have Catholic schools, while there are others that for whatever reason have closed them down. In these locations "the diocesan bishop has the responsibility of ensuring that such schools are established" (canon 802, paragraph 1).

There is one circumstance that releases the diocesan bishop from this burden. If schools "imbued with a Christian spirit" are found in the diocese, these schools may suffice for the education of Catholic children. Such schools are hard to find. With the clear separation of church and state in the Western world, public educational institutions have become hostile toward anything that smacks of religion.

The responsibility of the diocesan bishop to establish schools does not end with grade school and high school. The code also requires the diocesan bishop to work toward the "establishment of professional and technical schools, and of other schools catering for special needs" (canon 802, paragraph 2).

68. Who has say over the religion curriculum in our Catholic school?

Whenever a Catholic school takes on the responsibility of formation and education of students in the Catholic religion, it must rely on direction provided by Church leaders. The bishop serves as the foremost teacher of faith in his diocese. He is to regulate and watch over the Catholic formation and education in each school.

The law also claims influence over non-Catholic schools:

> The local Ordinary is to be careful that those who are appointed as teachers of religion in schools, even non-Catholic ones, are outstanding in true doctrine, in the witness of their Christian life, and in their teaching ability. (canon 804, paragraph 2)

The bishops of a nation may work together to produce guidelines on the formation and education of students, as well as materials that assist the Catholic school in its task. Nevertheless, with the massive amount of scientific and social change, especially regarding medical ethics and morality, teachers may have to scramble for resources that help to clarify the Catholic perspective. Catholic teachers should look to school board-appointed religion experts, their pastor, and their bishop to provide insight on difficult matters. The diocese may have resources, such as a Family Life Office or a board of experts who can assist the teacher.

69. A teacher in our grade school is teaching questionable topics. What can be done?

The diocesan bishop has the right to appoint, to approve, or to remove teachers of religion. So does a vicar general or episcopal vicar. "Teachers of religion" are teachers who have the responsibility in the school curriculum to teach aspects of the Catholic faith.

The law explains, "Teachers must be outstanding in true doctrine and uprightness of life" (canon 803, paragraph 2). If a teacher were to teach something that is at odds with "true doctrine," his or her employment could be terminated. As is the case in secular society, the teacher must be told of the problem and given a chance to correct the content of the teaching. However, if the error continues, the teacher can be fired.

If a teacher's life is not in keeping with Catholic morality, then his or her employment as a teacher of religion can be terminated. In accord with both canon law and civil law, the teacher must first be warned and given an opportunity to amend the behavior. Terminating employment is an unpleasant task, but the Church has the duty to ensure that children and youth are given accurate Catholic teaching and the best models of Christian life.

70. Can I be sure that a Catholic university is indeed Catholic in terms of academic teaching and way of life?

A university acquires the title *Catholic* through an official decree of a Church authority, usually a bishop. Such universities were usually founded by a diocese or religious order.

The strength of any university or college comes from its professors. Canon law states that these men and women are to be "suitable both in scientific and pedagogical expertise and in integrity of doctrine and uprightness of life" (canon 810, paragraph 1). If these requirements are found to be lacking, the professor is to be removed from teaching. Not only must professors be good teachers who know what they are to teach, but they must also live Christian lives.

There has always been a tension between the academic freedom of discovery and adherence to divine revelation. Genetic cloning is a contemporary issue that gives rise to this tension. The Catholic university must find a way to respect both disciplines, science and religion. In this light, the Catholic university has a lot to offer the academic community.

Ex corde ecclesiae, a Vatican document that was issued in 1990, maintains that all universities that use the title *Catholic* must have their professors recognized by the local bishop (or his equivalent). If a university does not comply, it may lose the title *Catholic*.

71. I've heard of pontifical universities and Catholic universities. Is there a difference?

Catholic universities can offer a large number of academic programs—for example, business, arts, science, engineering, and so on. Ecclesiastical or pontifical universities provide academic programs that meet the immediate needs of the Church. Canon law, for instance, is a discipline unique to the Church; Catholic theology is another such example.

If you study business, you might complete a bachelor of commerce degree, then a master's in business administration, and finally a doctorate in business. The Church has a similar structure. A primary study in theology results in a baccalaureate (or bachelor) degree, more advanced study results in a licentiate (or license), and further study leads to a doctorate. Only ecclesiastical universities and faculties can grant ecclesiastical degrees.

The pope establishes ecclesiastical universities and ecclesiastical faculties. This is why some ecclesiastical universities are referred to as pontifical universities. Given the nature of study in an ecclesiastical university, the Vatican is the body that regulates such institutions. Every ecclesiastical university or faculty must have its course of study approved by the Vatican.

72. There was a time when Catholic books had to be approved before publication. Is this still the case today?

If books or other publications take on the task of teaching the Catholic faith, they are subject to review before being printed. Canon law explains that this permission is made by a local ordinary (a bishop or a vicar general) after being reviewed by a censor (canons 824 and 830).

In each diocese there is to be a censor appointed to give judgments about books (canon 830). In order to assist smaller dioceses that may not have someone who has the expertise to review theological material, the nation's bishops may approve a list of censors to be used or even appoint a team of experts for the task.

A censor must give an opinion, in writing, to the one who requested the review. If the book is recommended for publishing, the local ordinary puts his name on the work and approves the publication. If the censor cannot recommend the material, the local ordinary must supply the author with the reasons why.

Much of this practice has gone by the wayside. However, if you want to be sure that the content of a book is in line with the teachings of the Church, look for an *imprimatur*, usually issued by a bishop, in the first few pages of the text. It may even tell you the name of the censor.

73. Are Catholics bound to one specific English translation of the Bible or does any translation suffice?

The books of the Old and New Testaments were written in a variety of languages, for the most part Hebrew and Greek. Whenever the Church encountered a new language, a translation of the Bible was needed.

Since Sacred Scripture is the foundation on which the Church is built, one can appreciate the care the Church takes in ensuring that appropriate language translations are available to Catholics throughout the world. Sacred Scripture has informed and continues to inform the Church's tradition, so bishops, priests, deacons, biblical scholars, theologians, and other experts need accurate translations with which to meditate, discern, and make decisions that impact Christians in the modern age.

There are two settings in which translations of the Bible are used: the public setting of worship and the private setting of prayer or study. Canon law requires that whenever a translation of Sacred Scripture is proposed for Catholics, it must be approved by an office of the Vatican or by a conference of bishops (canon 825). Since the drafting of the *Code of Canon Law*, the Vatican has retained the right to approve translations for public worship.

74. Can our parish publish a prayer book for members of the parish?

Lex orandi, lex credendi is an ancient Latin saying that means, "The way we pray must reflect what we believe." It's wonderful when people discover a particular prayer that encourages their faith and worship of God.

The Church is rich with prayers given to us by Christ and the saints. We have prayers that have been around since the inception of the Church. Some prayers come directly from Scripture. Other prayers have been developed through the centuries of Christianity, such as the rosary. These so-called "traditional" prayers have stood the test of time. They reflect our belief in God.

Still, there are prayers that are created in our contemporary experience of God. Parishes have prayers for parish missions, and prayer groups find prayers born out of their very act of praying. The wealth of ways to praise God is something the Church cherishes.

From time to time a parish community or a prayer group within a parish wants to collect and publish a book of prayers. Some of these prayers may not reflect the doctrine of our faith; people of good intention may make theological errors. For this reason, a book of prayers that is to be printed for distribution to other Catholics must first have the approval of the bishop or vicar general in the diocese. The obligation to have such a proposal reviewed is matched with the obligation of diocesan authorities to actually review it!

CHAPTER 9

Baptism

75. What is the Code's basic teaching concerning baptism?

The teaching is contained in canon 849: → *a theological canon*

> Baptism, the gateway to the sacraments, is necessary for salvation, either by actual reception or at least by desire. By it people are freed from sins, are born again as children of God and, made like to Christ by an indelible character, are incorporated into the Church. It is validly conferred only by a washing in real water with the proper form and words.

As one can see, this is a theological canon. It purposely expresses a number of key theological truths concerning the sacrament of baptism. For instance, baptism is "the gateway to the other sacraments." This means that one must first receive baptism before one can lawfully (and validly) receive the other sacraments. Thus, one's sacramental life within the Church begins with the reception of baptism.

Additionally, baptism imprints an "indelible character" upon one's soul. This means that once baptized, one is baptized for life. One cannot be "unbaptized," nor can baptism be repeated once it is validly received, for through baptism one becomes a Christian and is incorporated into the universal Church. Thus baptism, or its desire (whether implicit or explicit), is required for salvation.

Finally, only real water may be used, accompanied by the proper baptismal formula: "I baptize you in the name of the Father, and of the Son, and of the Holy Spirit."

76. Who may baptize an infant if the danger of death presents itself?

Canon 867 — Emergency Baptism

The Church does not wish anybody to pass into the next life without the grace of baptism. Therefore, canon 867, paragraph 2, states that an infant in danger of death "is to be baptized without any delay." One need not even be a priest or a deacon to baptize. When an infant is in danger of death, any Catholic, baptized Christian, or even nonbaptized person may validly baptize. What is required is that the individual performing the baptism intends to do what the Church requires, uses real water, and pronounces the words "I baptize you in the name of the Father, and of the Son, and of the Holy Spirit. Amen."

If there is any chance that a danger of death exists, the emergency baptism should be performed. Additionally, if there is serious doubt about whether the infant is still living, the formula for conditional baptism should be used: "On condition that you are alive, I baptize you in the name of the Father, and of the Son, and of the Holy Spirit. Amen."

Moreover, the canonical obligation to baptize in an emergency applies to miscarried babies. And while the Church remains steadfast in condemning abortion as a grave evil, its victims should be baptized if at all possible. This obligation is found in canon 871: "Aborted fetuses, if they are alive, are to be baptized, in so far as this is possible."

77. If a child is baptized, whose consent is needed? The child's? That of the parents? Or that of both the parents and the child?

An adult must consent to his or her own baptism. An infant lacks the necessary use of reason to consent to baptism, so the parents or legal guardians consent on his or her behalf. These two scenarios are clear to most people.

Yet whose consent is needed to baptize a child who has reached the age of reason? According to the first paragraph of canon 852, "The provisions of the canons on adult baptism apply to all those who, having ceased to be infants, have reached the use of reason." Thus a child who has reached the use of reason but is still considered a minor must consent to the baptism before receiving this sacrament. Under canon 97, a child is considered to have reached the use of reason after the completion of his or her seventh year.

Yet what about children who have completed their seventh year of age but because of mental or cognitive disability have not attained the use of reason? An example would be a child who suffers from a severe form of Down's Syndrome. The second paragraph of canon 852 states, "One who is incapable of personal responsibility is regarded as an infant even in regard to baptism." Therefore, in such situations the consent of the parents or legal guardian is necessary.

78. Must one receive any catechetical formation prior to receiving baptism?

It depends. According to canon 851, an adult candidate for baptism "is to be admitted to the catechumenate and, as far as possible, brought through the various stages to sacramental initiation." The catechumenate is a process of catechesis, prayer, and discernment. Through this process a candidate is introduced to the Catholic faith, and his or her resolve is tested. Of course, should danger of death or some other grave necessity threaten, the process would be shortened to allow the adult candidate to receive baptism.

Obviously an infant cannot undertake the process of catechesis and discernment required of an adult seeking baptism into the Catholic Church. Therefore, as canon 851 continues, "the parents of a child who is to be baptized, and those who are to undertake the office of sponsors, are to be suitably instructed on the meaning of the sacrament and the obligations attaching to it." The parents and godparents receive instruction not only on the sacrament of baptism but also on their obligations to raise the child in the Catholic faith.

79. What about the mentally and cognitively challenged? Does canon law see a duty for pastors to catechize and instruct Catholics with special needs?

Canon 777 provides an appropriate answer to this question:

> In a special way the parish priest is to ensure, in accordance with the norms laid down by the diocesan Bishop, that...an

adequate catechesis is given for the celebration of the sacraments [and]... as far as their condition allows, catechetical formation is given to the mentally and physically handicapped.

In other words, the pastor of a parish should ensure that Catholics
with special needs receive ongoing catechesis insofar as they are
capable. Of course, they may not comprehend or retain knowledge of
the Church's teaching at the same level as others their age. Often
even the most elementary catechesis must be repeated during the
course of their lifetime. Nevertheless, the Second Vatican Council
calls all Catholics to live a life of holiness and to deepen one's knowledge of the Catholic faith. This includes Catholics with special needs.

80. Are parents required to use the name of a saint when giving their child a baptismal name?

While giving one's child the name of a saint is a pious practice in
many parts of the world, it is no longer essential under canon law.
This does not mean, however, that any name may be given to the
child. Rather, as canon 855 clearly states, "parents, sponsors and
parish priests are to take care that a name is not given which is foreign to Christian sentiment."

The obligation to choose a name consistent with the Christian
faith falls upon parents, godparents, and pastors. The saints provide
a vast reservoir of names from which to draw, but other names are
also consistent with Christian sentiment. For example, Faith, Hope,
and Charity are popular choices. These names of the three theological virtues are certainly consistent with Christian sentiment.
Therefore, canon 855 permits their use.

81. Must one receive baptism on a Sunday or at the Easter vigil? Or does any day of the week suffice?

Canon 856 states: "Though baptism may be celebrated on any day,
it is recommended that normally it be celebrated on a Sunday or, if
possible, on the vigil of Easter." Sunday is the day upon which our

Lord rose from the dead, and baptism symbolizes our death and resurrection with Christ. Thus Sunday is particularly symbolic in terms of its relationship to baptism. Similarly, the Easter Vigil is appropriate in terms of symbolism, because on this day the Catholic faithful focus in anticipation on Christ's resurrection.

Nevertheless, these are simply the Church's recommendations. Canon law in no way binds us to receive baptism on these days, and there is no canonical prohibition against administering baptism on any other day of the week. In fact, the text of the canon clearly states the opposite: "Baptism may be celebrated on any day."

Of course, outside of the danger of death or any other grave necessity, a proposed date for baptism should be agreeable to the parents, the godparents, and the pastor.

82. Must my child be baptized in a church, or can we have the baptism at home?

The first paragraph of canon 857 is clear: "Apart from a case of necessity, the proper place for baptism is a church or an oratory." The Code of Canon Law deliberately avoids defining the term case of necessity, since various scenarios that canon law cannot anticipate may present themselves. Thus, how to interpret this canon is left to the discretion of the individual who may be called to baptize in a case of necessity.

Baptism is a public act of worship by the Church. The individual receiving baptism is publicly welcomed into communion with Christ and the Church. A church or oratory is the most appropriate place to receive baptism, since these are sacred places reserved for acts of public worship.

This is in keeping with the first paragraph of canon 860, "Apart from a case of necessity, baptism is not to be conferred in private houses, unless the local Ordinary should for a grave reason permit it." In canonical parlance, the local ordinary is the diocesan bishop, the vicar general, or an episcopal vicar with jurisdiction over the person being baptized. The responsibility for judging whether or not a reason is sufficiently grave is left to the local ordinary.

83. I want to become Catholic. I was baptized and confirmed in the Methodist Church. Do I have to be baptized and confirmed again?

Some sacraments are not repeated. The sacraments of baptism, confirmation, and holy orders leave an "indelible mark on the soul." The *Code of Canon Law* chooses to say they "imprint a character" (canon 845, paragraph 1). The point is that the recipients of such sacraments are fundamentally changed to the extent that repeating these sacraments is simply not necessary; in fact, it is prohibited.

Most Protestant denominations celebrate baptism validly. This means that they baptize with water, in the name of the Father, and of the Son, and of the Holy Spirit. The Protestant official conducting the baptism correctly understands the Blessed Trinity and intends to perform the baptism. This means that such a baptism is performed in the same way as in the Catholic Church, and it is valid. Once baptism is validly given, it is not repeated.

Confirmation is a different matter. In order for confirmation to be valid, special oil called chrism, blessed by a bishop, needs to be used. Protestant denominations do not confirm with this sacred oil, so what Protestants call "confirmation" is not valid in the Catholic Church. It can therefore be said that most non-Catholic Christians must receive confirmation but not baptism when they become Catholic. See Chapter 10 for more information on the sacrament of confirmation.

84. I can find only one godparent for my child. Is this OK?

It is customary for people to choose two godparents for their children. When we think of godparents, a godfather and a godmother come to mind. The law, however, states, "In so far as possible, a person being baptized is to be assigned a sponsor" (canon 872), and, "One sponsor, male or female, is sufficient" (canon 873). If there is only one godparent for the baptism, this person must be a Catholic.

The law permits two sponsors, "one of each sex" (canon 873), but it does not provide the option of having more than two. The priest or deacon performing the baptism does not have to acknowledge more than two sponsors, one male and one female. Some cultures have the practice of designating more than two godparents. While this is fine, only two godparents will be recorded in the baptismal register.

85. What is required of a godparent?) W,TNess es Christian

Canon law talks about two types of godparents: "sponsors" and "witnesses." A sponsor is a Catholic, and a witness is a baptized Christian of another denomination. This distinction is made since a witness cannot be expected to assist in raising a Catholic child in the Catholic faith. The child must have at least one sponsor as a godparent.

Canon law lists a number of necessary qualities for the sponsor:

- The parents of the child to be baptized (or the adult to be baptized) must appoint the sponsor.
- The sponsor should be at least sixteen years of age, unless there is good reason for choosing someone under this age. The Church wants to be sure to provide a role model who is mature and resolved to practice the Catholic faith.
- For this same reason, the sponsor must be a fully initiated Catholic. He or she must have received the sacraments of baptism, Holy Communion, and confirmation. He or she must live a life in keeping with the faith and moral teachings of the Church.
- The sponsor cannot be a parent of the child, since parents have their own special role; however, grandparents are certainly acceptable.

Canon law does not list qualities for witnesses, but it would seem that similar expectations exist. Witnesses need to be baptized, be of an appropriate age, practice the Christian faith, and live a life that is in keeping with the faith and moral teachings of the Church.

86. Can a Catholic be a godparent in the baptism of a Protestant?

Since a Protestant can be a godparent in a Catholic baptism, Church law permits a Catholic to be a godparent at the baptism of a Protestant. This go-ahead is not found in the *Code of Canon Law* but in another important document, which was released by the Holy See in 1993, *Directory for the Application of Principles and Norms on Ecumenism* (Pontifical Council for Promoting Christian Unity).

A Catholic invited to be a godparent to a Protestant acts only as a witness to the baptism. Such a distinction is made because a Catholic cannot help direct someone in the ways of a Protestant denomination but can merely be a witness to the Christian faith. In light of this, the Catholic witness to a Protestant baptism should ensure that the other godparent is a member of the Protestant denomination in which the baptism takes place and decline the invitation if no such person is designated.

The Catholic Church shares much more in common with Orthodox Churches than with Protestant denominations. The Orthodox Churches have validly ordained priests and bishops and, like Catholics, observe seven sacraments. In light of these similarities, Orthodox people can act as sponsors in the baptism of a Catholic and vice versa.

CHAPTER 10

The Sacrament of Confirmation

87. What is the basic understanding of the sacrament of confirmation held by canonists?

Canon 879 summarizes the Church's basic theological teaching concerning the sacrament of confirmation:

> The sacrament of confirmation confers a character. By it the baptized continue their path of Christian initiation. They are enriched with the gift of the Holy Spirit, and are more closely linked to the Church. They are made strong and more firmly obliged by word and deed to witness to Christ and to spread and defend the faith.

This canon reveals a number of key theological truths about this sacrament. First of all, along with baptism and ordination, confirmation is one of three sacraments that confer a permanent mark on one's soul. Additionally, confirmation is among the three sacraments of initiation, the other two being baptism and reception of the Holy Eucharist. Only after these three sacraments are received is one considered fully initiated into the Christian faith.

Finally, the purpose of the sacrament of confirmation is to strengthen the individual in the Holy Spirit and allow him or her to act more strongly as a witness to Christ's gospel. Thus confirmation is closely linked to baptism, in that it allows one to more readily share the faith one receives at baptism.

88. My daughter was baptized Eastern Catholic. Why can't she be confirmed with her Latin Catholic classmates?

The practice within the Eastern Catholic Churches is to administer all three sacraments of initiation to infants. These sacraments are baptism, chrismation (or confirmation), and reception of the Holy Eucharist. According to your daughter's baptismal certificate, she already received confirmation at the Eastern Catholic parish.

As previously mentioned, confirmation is a sacrament that imprints an indelible character upon one's soul. The character is permanent, and one may receive it only once. The first paragraph of canon 889 specifically stipulates, "Every baptized who is not confirmed, and only such a person, is capable of receiving confirmation."

Because most Catholic schools within North America operate under the auspices of the Latin Catholic hierarchy, this can be a touchy pastoral issue for Eastern Catholic children when the time comes for confirmation. Nobody wants to feel left out, particularly at such a young age. Nevertheless, any attempt to reconfirm an Eastern Catholic child is both invalid and highly unlawful.

As a practical solution to this pastoral dilemma, many canonists suggest that the Latin parish invite their Eastern Catholic children to participate as altar servers during their classmates' confirmation liturgy.

89. Is a special oil used in the sacrament of confirmation? Or does any oil suffice?

There is indeed a special oil used for confirmation; it is called chrism. Although any vegetable oil will suffice, by custom chrism derives from olive oil mixed with balsam. The diocesan bishop consecrates this oil on Holy Thursday at the Mass of Holy Chrism.

This brings us to the second paragraph of canon 880: "The chrism to be used in the sacrament of confirmation must have been consecrated by a Bishop, even when the sacrament is administered by a priest." In other words, because of the historic connection between the diocesan bishop and the sacrament of confirmation, only holy chrism should be used when administering this sacrament.

Nevertheless, another vegetable oil may be substituted for olive oil when certain exceptional circumstances present themselves. For validity, the vegetable oil substituted must also be consecrated by a bishop. The use of unconsecrated vegetable oil invalidates the attempted sacrament.

90. When and where should the sacrament of confirmation be celebrated?

It is desirable that the sacrament of confirmation be celebrated in a church and indeed during Mass. However, for a just and reasonable cause it may be celebrated apart from Mass and in any fitting place (canon 881).

Like the other sacraments, confirmation is part of the Church's public prayer. Therefore it should be celebrated in a sacred place reserved for public worship. Additionally, because of the connection between confirmation and the Holy Eucharist as sacraments of initiation, confirmation should be celebrated during Mass. This is the ideal presented by the *Code of Canon Law*.

Nevertheless, the canon recognizes that the sacrament of confirmation is not always administered under ideal circumstances. Thus when a just and reasonable cause presents itself, canon law allows the sacrament of confirmation to be celebrated apart from the Mass in any fitting place. The code does not define the term *just and reasonable cause*. This is left to the judgment of the priest or bishop called to administer the sacrament under circumstances that are less than ideal. Similarly, the expression *any fitting place* is left to the pastoral discretion of the minister.

For example, suppose a baptized Protestant lies dying in the hospital and wishes to convert to Catholicism. Her medical condition confines her to the hospital bed, and it would be very inconvenient for the priest to celebrate Mass in her hospital room. The priest may still confirm this woman in spite of the fact that such a celebration of the sacrament would take place outside of a church and apart from the Mass.

91. Who is the ordinary minister of confirmation in the Latin Church?

While Eastern Catholics have their own laws concerning this matter, canon 882 specifies, "The ordinary minister of confirmation is a Bishop." Even in the Roman rite the bishop's capacity to administer this sacrament is by no means exclusive. Canon 882 continues, "A priest can also validly confer this sacrament if he has the faculty to do so, either from the universal law or by way of a special grant from the competent authority." This faculty may come from the competent authority, which is usually the diocesan bishop, or it may come from the law itself.

For example, suppose the diocesan bishop must undergo emergency medical treatment around the time that several parishes have scheduled their confirmations. Moreover, these confirmations cannot be rescheduled without seriously inconveniencing Christ's faithful. Acting as the competent authority, the diocesan bishop may therefore delegate the faculty to confirm to the vicar general, the individual pastor, or some other priest of the diocese.

On the other hand, canon 883 provides several instances when the law itself allows the priest to administer the sacrament of confirmation without obtaining the faculty from the diocesan bishop. For example, "In respect of those in danger of death, the parish priest or indeed any priest...have, by law, the faculty to administer confirmation."

92. Our diocese has set the minimum age for confirmation at twelve. Can my toddler receive confirmation if the danger of death presents itself?

Baptism is not the only sacrament available to infants and children when in danger of death. Under such circumstances Catholic parents also have the canonical right to see their children confirmed. This is clearly stated in canon 891:

> The sacrament of confirmation is to be conferred on the faithful at about the age of discretion, unless...there is a danger of death or, in the judgment of the minister, a grave reason suggests otherwise.

In short, when a child's life is seriously endangered, other than baptism all the usual requirements for confirmation cease. This would include diocesan legislation setting a minimum age for confirmation.

93. My son suffers from a severe form of autism. His condition prevents him from fulfilling our diocese's catechetical requirements for the reception of confirmation. Can he still be confirmed?

The Church reminds us, both in the first paragraph of canon 889 and in article 1306 of the *Catechism of the Catholic Church*, that those who have been baptized "can and should" receive the sacrament of confirmation. Canon 890 specifies that parents and pastors are to instruct the faithful with regard to the reception of this sacrament, and canon 889, paragraph 2, clearly states that the individual seeking confirmation must have the "use of reason." Nevertheless, the inability to receive the proper catechesis does not exclude one from this sacrament. In fact, catechesis can and should be adapted to suit particular needs.

In addressing these special circumstances, the Bishops in the United States, under guideline 16 of their *Guidelines for Celebration of the Sacraments with Persons with Disabilities*, encourage Catholics with special needs to request the sacraments. If the individual lacks the requisite mental or cognitive capacity to make this request, the parent or legal guardian may petition on behalf of the child for the administration of the sacrament. Thus the American bishops guard against any rigid application of the law, opting instead to follow the canonical principle of "favors are to be multiplied, and burdens restricted."

94. I am the parent of a special needs child and have read several of your commentaries concerning special needs children and access to the sacraments. However, I am having a difficult time convincing our parish's director of religious education. Can you please help me?

Allow us to digress from the purely canonical for a moment and speak personally. While both of us have dealt with this issue in the past, Pete is particularly experienced in helping parents of special needs children to resolve this issue.

In our experience, the parents of special needs children are not the only ones intimidated by this issue. Because of the numerous changes to the law since the closing of the Second Vatican Council, pastors and directors of religious education are often unsure of themselves when facing this pastoral dilemma. Please respect where they are coming from, while maintaining that your Catholic child has a canonical right to receive the sacraments.

The path to vindicating the sacramental rights of your special needs child is fraught with many canonical subtleties. Pete is more than happy to help you navigate these waters. He invites any parent or legal guardian of a special needs child to contact him through the International Order of Alhambra. This is a Catholic family organization dedicated to serving the needs of the mentally and cognitively challenged. Please visit the website www.OrderAlhambra.org or call 1-800-478-2946.

95. What are the qualifications of a sponsor of a candidate for confirmation? Must the sponsor for confirmation be one of the baptismal godparents?

Canon 893 answers both of these questions. The first paragraph states, "A person who would undertake the office of sponsor must fulfill the conditions mentioned in canon 874." This is a reference to the conditions one must fulfill to be a godparent at baptism:

- The sponsor must be appointed by the individual, the individual's parents, or the pastor and have the intention of fulfilling this role.
- The sponsor must be at least sixteen years of age.
- The sponsor must be confirmed and have received the Holy Eucharist and must practice the Catholic faith.
- The sponsor must not be subject to any canonical penalties such as interdict or excommunication.
- The sponsor must not be the mother or the father of the individual receiving confirmation.

A person needs only one sponsor for the sacrament of confirmation. The second paragraph of canon 893 continues, "It is desirable that the sponsor chosen be the one who undertook this role at baptism." However, this is simply "desirable" whenever possible; it is by no means essential. The individual receiving confirmation is free to choose another suitable candidate.

CHAPTER 11

The Celebration of the Holy Eucharist

96. Are the canons pertaining to the Holy Eucharist presented in light of the Church's theology of the Eucharist?

Yes. In fact, the first canon under the title "Eucharist," canon 897, states:

> The most august sacrament is the blessed Eucharist, in which Christ the Lord himself is contained, offered and received, and by which the Church continually lives and grows. The eucharistic Sacrifice, the memorial of the death and resurrection of the Lord, in which the Sacrifice of the cross is forever perpetuated, is the summit and the source of all worship and Christian life. By means of it the unity of God's people is signified and brought about, and the building up of the body of Christ is perfected. The other sacraments and all the eclesiastical works of the apostolate are bound up with, and directed to, the blessed Eucharist.

Canon lawyers refer to this as a theological canon. Its purpose is not to give us a particular law or practice but rather to set the theological scene through which all other canons pertaining to the Holy Eucharist will be interpreted. In short, this canon stresses certain theological principles that our Holy Father wants us to keep in mind when reading the canons on the Holy Eucharist. It is like a pair of glasses that helps us focus on what is important within the canons. We discover within this canon that Christ is contained within the Holy Eucharist, that he offers himself up to God the Father through the Holy Sacrifice of the Mass, and that we receive his Body, Blood, soul, and divinity. We learn that the Mass perpetuates Christ's sacrifice on the cross for our sins. We also see a repetition of Vatican II's great theological insights, including the fact that the Eucharist is the source and summit of Catholic worship and Catholic spirituality. This is not an invention of the *Code of Canon Law* but a repetition of what the Second Vatican Council teaches in its "Constitution on the Sacred Liturgy," *Sacrosanctum Concilium.*

Finally, this canon reminds us that all we do as Catholics ought to be directed to the Holy Eucharist, because all of our good works as Catholics are intrinsically linked to this Most Holy Sacrament.

97. Does canon law speak of the reverence that Catholics should have toward the Holy Eucharist?

Yes. Canon 898 specifically states,

> Christ's faithful are to hold the blessed Eucharist in the highest honor. They should take an active part in the celebration of the most august Sacrifice; they should receive the sacrament with great devotion and frequently, and should reverence it with the greatest adoration. In explaining the doctrine of this sacrament, pastors of souls are assiduously to instruct the faithful about their obligation in this regard.

This canon covers both theological and practical matters. As baptized Catholics, we are to hold the Holy Eucharist in the highest honor because the Eucharist is the real presence of our Lord Jesus Christ. For this same reason, the Church calls us to actively participate in the Holy Sacrifice of the Mass. We should receive the sacrament often, always approaching it with great devotion. In fact, we are to adore the Holy Eucharist—meaning to offer the Eucharist the worship due to God alone.

Finally, this canon requires priests and bishops to instruct Catholics under their care in all these obligations toward the Blessed Sacrament.

98. What does canon law teach about the celebration of the Holy Eucharist?

The first paragraph of canon 899 offers insight concerning the celebration of the Holy Eucharist:

The celebration of the Eucharist is an action of Christ himself and of the Church. In it Christ the Lord, through the ministry of the priest, offers himself, substantially present under the appearances of bread and wine, to God the Father, and gives himself as spiritual nourishment to the faithful who are associated with him in his offering.

This introductory canon nicely blends the theology of the Eucharist with the more practical elements of the Eucharist. To begin, the celebration of the Eucharist—or the Mass, as it is more commonly called—is an action of Christ himself. For it is Christ who offers himself to God the Father in atonement for our sins. Yet Christ performs this action through the priest, with whom we are joined during the Mass. And thus the Mass is also an action of the Church, for through the eucharistic action we join together as Christ's Mystical Body. Together with our head Jesus Christ, the eucharistic sacrifice is offered to God the Father.

We discover from this canon that Christ offers himself to us as well. For through the Eucharist we receive the Body, Blood, soul, and divinity of our Lord Jesus Christ, our spiritual nourishment.

99. Does canon law teach anything about the Mass as a communal celebration?

The second paragraph of canon 899 states,

> In the eucharistic assembly the people of God are called together under the presidency of the Bishop or of a priest under his authority, who acts in the person of Christ. All the faithful present, whether clerics or laypeople, unite to participate in their own way, according to their various orders and liturgical roles.

This canon harmonizes the doctrine of the Catholic faith with the practice thereof. When we gather to celebrate the Mass, it is always under the direction of the diocesan bishop or a priest approved by him. During the Mass the priest acts in the person of Christ. This is what the Church means when it refers to the bishop or priest as an *alter Christus*, meaning "another Christ."

Nevertheless, all Catholics are called to participate in the Holy Sacrifice of the Mass. Lay Catholics may fulfill various other liturgical roles during the celebration.

100. Who can bring about the Holy Sacrifice of the Mass?

Canon 900 provides the clear answer in its first paragraph: "The only minister who, in the person of Christ, can bring into being the sacrament of the Eucharist, is a validly ordained priest."

As previously noted, canon law distinguishes between lawfulness and validity. This canon concerns the validity of the sacrament. If one who is not a validly ordained priest should attempt the consecration, that individual's actions are both unlawful and invalid. The consecration simply does not take place.

Also note that the word used for "priest" in the Latin text of canon 900 is *sacerdos,* which includes all priests—from the assistant pastor at a small country parish to the supreme pontiff, the bishop of Rome. (The word *presbytos,* on the other hand, refers to any priest who is not also a bishop.)

101. What if a validly ordained priest is not in good standing with the Church? May he still celebrate the Mass?

This question concerns the lawfulness of the priest's celebration of the Mass rather than the validity.

The second paragraph of canon 900 says, "Any priest who is not debarred by canon law may lawfully celebrate the Eucharist, provided the provisions of the following canons are observed."

As one can discern from this canon, the celebrant at Mass must be in good standing with the Church. For example, canons 1331 to 1333 outline the canonical censures of excommunication, interdict, and suspension. A priest who labors under any of these three penalties is not permitted by the Church to lawfully celebrate Mass.

→ illegal

If a priest chooses to ignore these penalties and celebrate Mass anyway, his Mass is valid but illicit. An example is a Mass celebrated by the bishops of the Society of St. Pius X (SSPX), whom the Church has excommunicated. Their Masses are valid in that transubstantiation really takes place during the consecration. Nevertheless, because the four SSPX bishops labor under the penalty of excommunication, the Catholic Church considers their celebrations of the Mass unlawful.

102. Our priest not only changes words and phrases at the Mass but also adds his own prayers and "mini-rituals." Can he do this?

One of the marvelous aspects of the Mass is that wherever you go in the world, even though the language may differ, the order of the Mass is the same. Prayers in other languages are familiar to the ear because of their cadence and sound. The Roman Catholic Church has not always emphasized uniformity in liturgy, but it certainly does today.

The liturgical books from which the Mass and other forms of liturgy are celebrated provide some flexibility for additions, omissions, and substitutions. We worship as finite beings and bring our day-to-day lives with all their struggles and joys to Mass every week. Our worship of God should not be disconnected from these experiences, and in attempts to make the liturgy more grounded in or more appealing to the lives of the faithful, the liturgical books permit some change. Nevertheless, the rule is to not deviate from the text of the liturgy.

With this in mind, canon 846, paragraph 1, explains that the liturgical books are "to be faithfully followed in the celebration of the sacraments." As a consequence, "no one may on a personal initiative add or omit or alter anything in those books." Those who preside over the liturgy are restricted to the text of the liturgical books, and deviations need to be authorized by the text itself.

It should be noted that some approved prayers and rituals are rarely used and may be unfamiliar to some of us. So what you consider a deviation may actually be lawful.

103. My Jewish aunt is undergoing surgery. Can I have a Mass offered for her even though she is not a Catholic? Does the fact that she is still living make any difference?

Although this would have been a problem in previous times, there is no longer any prohibition against having a Mass offered for a non-Catholic. Nor is there a requirement that an individual be deceased before one may have a Mass offered for him or her. As canon 901 clearly states, "A priest is entitled to offer Mass for anyone, living or dead." In fact, the authors themselves have often had Masses offered for the living.

One should never underestimate God's mercy; nor should one underestimate the efficacy of the Holy Sacrifice of the Mass offered for the living or the dead. Indeed, no prayer is wasted in God's eyes. While these theological truths are not strictly spelled out in the *Code of Canon Law*, theology is at the root of every canon.

104. How often should a priest celebrate Mass?

While there is no prescribed frequency within the *Code of Canon Law*, canon 904 offers the following guidance:

> Remembering always that in the mystery of the eucharistic Sacrifice the work of redemption is continually being carried out, priests are to celebrate frequently. Indeed, daily celebration is earnestly recommended, because, even if it should not be possible to have the faithful present, it is an action of Christ and of the Church in which priests fulfill their principal role.

In putting the Church's theological insights into practice, this canon provides an excellent example of theology informing canon law. On the basis of theology we discern that a priest is ordained to celebrate the sacraments—among which the Eucharist enjoys a certain primacy. All the other sacraments are directed toward the Mass. Thus the canon itself refers to the celebration of the Eucharist as the priest's principal, or most important, role. It only makes sense, then, that canon 904 enthusiastically recommends that priests celebrate the Mass daily when possible.

105. Since the Eucharist is central to our spiritual life as Catholics, how often should the priest celebrate Mass in a given day?

Basically a priest should celebrate Mass only once a day. As the first paragraph of canon 905 makes clear, "Apart from those cases in which the law allows him to celebrate or concelebrate the Eucharist a number of times on the same day, a priest may not celebrate more than once a day." Because of the priest's many other pastoral duties, a priest who celebrates the Mass more than once a day would eventually risk exhaustion.

There are some exceptions to this rule, which are noted in canon 905. We will deal with these in subsequent questions. Once a day is the norm.

While many canonists differ among themselves as to where this custom originates, the present authors will venture their own speculations. According to the Second Vatican Council, the celebration of the Mass is the central point of our spiritual life. This applies in particular to priests, who are to make the celebration of Mass the focal point of their ministry and daily spiritual activity. Thus, in restricting a priest to one celebration of Mass each day, the canon really reinforces two ideas: (1) All of a priest's daily ministry should lead him closer to our Lord in the Holy Eucharist; and (2) a priest's entire ministry should flow from the graces he receives during his daily celebration of the Mass.

106. Why restrict a priest to one daily celebration of the Mass when there is such a scarcity of priests in our diocese? Should the laity not also enjoy the opportunity to assist at daily Mass?

The answer to your second question is yes! Thus the first paragraph of canon 905 is not absolute. Its second paragraph states,

> If there is a scarcity of priests, the local Ordinary may for a
> good reason allow priests to celebrate twice in one day or

even, if pastoral need requires it, three times on Sundays or holy days of obligation.

There are two things one must keep in mind when interpreting this portion of the canon. First, who is the local ordinary? Although most Catholics use this term interchangeably with the term *diocesan bishop*, the local ordinary can be the vicar general or an episcopal vicar appointed by the diocesan bishop (see canon 134, paragraph 1). Provided the diocesan bishop has not stated otherwise, either of these individuals may also give a priest permission to celebrate Mass more than once each day.

Secondly, what "good reason" allows a priest to celebrate Mass more than once each day? It could be a shortage of priests within a diocese, a great number of faithful who wish to come to daily Mass, or any other circumstance both the local ordinary and the priest view as significant. Note that it need not be a serious reason or an exceptional reason but simply a good reason. Again, the *Code of Canon Law* does not define the expression *for a good reason*. This is deliberate, as the *Code* generally trusts in the common sense of the Church's bishops and priests when interpreting this particular canon.

107. May a priest celebrate Mass without the presence of at least one member of the Catholic faithful? What if no other Catholics are available to assist him in the celebration of the Eucharist?

As canon 906 states, "a priest may not celebrate the eucharistic Sacrifice without the participation of at least one of the faithful, unless there is a good and reasonable cause for doing so."

As one can discern from the language with which it is written, this canon is more a reminder of Catholic principle than a strict rule to follow. The real purpose of the canon is to remind the priest that Mass is not one of his private devotions but rather the source and the summit of the Church's public prayer. Thus the entire Church participates in the Mass.

Again, the interpretation of the expression *a good and reasonable cause* is left to the discernment of the priest. The Church trusts that if an individual is ordained to the priesthood, his judgment is reasonably sound. A good reason may be anything from the desire to offer a Mass for a special intention when there is no Mass scheduled to being on retreat, where there is nobody to assist at the Mass.

Where there is no other Catholic directly present, it is commonly understood that the angels and saints participate in the priest's Mass. Therefore the universal Church is still present at the Mass offered by the lone priest.

108. In the absence of a priest or a bishop, may a deacon, religious sister, or layperson preside over the Mass?

Absolutely not. Previously we noted that each member of Christ's faithful has a role to play within the liturgy. It is important that roles not be confused. Canon 907 makes clear:

> In the celebration of the Eucharist, deacons and lay persons are not permitted to say the prayers, especially the eucharistic prayer, nor to perform the actions which are proper to the celebrating priest.

This prohibition is of extreme importance when it comes to the eucharistic prayers. Returning to canon 900, only a priest or bishop has the power to consecrate the bread and wine into the Body, Blood, soul, and divinity of our Lord. If a deacon or layman were to recite the eucharistic prayers during the liturgy, transubstantiation would not take place. Hence the Mass would be invalid and not merely unlawful.

109. Who is the minister of Holy Communion? What is an extraordinary minister of Holy Communion?

In response to this first question, the first paragraph of canon 910 states, "The ordinary minister of holy communion is a Bishop, a priest or a deacon." This minister is not necessarily the same individual who consecrates the bread and wine into the Body and Blood of our Lord. Of course, the priest celebrating the Mass should also be a minister of Holy Communion, but others may assist him in administering the sacrament to Christ's faithful.

Most Catholics have attended a Mass where, due to the large crowd, it would be nearly impossible for the priest to administer the sacrament without needlessly prolonging the Mass. Therefore the second paragraph of canon 910 continues, "The extraordinary minister of holy communion is an acolyte, or another of Christ's faithful deputed in accordance with canon 230, paragraph 3."

In short, canon law is very reasonable. The Church allows, when needed, extraordinary ministers of Holy Communion to assist the priest. Under such circumstances, the extraordinary minister of Holy Communion should be an acolyte. But as one reads in canon 230, paragraph 3, if sufficient acolytes are not available, any baptized Catholic who is present may be deputed to act as an extraordinary minister of Holy Communion.

110. Ordinarily, who has the right to bring Holy Communion to the sick and the dying?

According to the first paragraph of canon 911,

> The duty and right to bring the blessed Eucharist to the sick as Viaticum belongs to the parish priest, to assistant priests, to chaplains and, in respect of all who are in the house, to the community Superior in clerical religious institutes or societies of apostolic life.

This first paragraph of the canon is fairly self-explanatory. Basically, it establishes who has the right to bring viaticum to the sick. *Viaticum* comes from an old Latin expression meaning "food for the journey." It should not be confused with the sacrament of the sick, otherwise known as extreme unction. *Viaticum* is what we call the Eucharist when our Lord is brought to an individual suffering from serious illness or in danger of death. It should not be confused with regular Communion calls to the sick and elderly. Thus death is "the journey" referred to in this expression.

In the case of an individual who does not belong to a religious order, both the duty and the right to bring viaticum belongs to the parish priest, any of his assistants, or a chaplain if the sick person is staying at an institution such as a hospital or a nursing home. If the sick person happens to be a religious, in addition to those individuals previously mentioned, the religious superior also has both the right and the duty to bring this person viaticum.

111. What happens if none of the individuals mentioned in the previous question are available? Can the sick and the dying still receive viaticum?

These are important questions, since nobody should pass on to the next life without the comfort of our Lord in the Holy Eucharist. Thus the second paragraph of canon 911 continues,

> In a case of necessity, or with the permission at least presumed of the parish priest, chaplain or Superior, who must subsequently be notified, any priest or other minister of holy communion must do this.

As the Church is called by Christ to be merciful, our Lord's mercy must be reflected in canon law. The second paragraph of canon 911 is a good example of such. In a state of necessity—in other words, should a serious situation arise in which no priest is available to bring viaticum to the dying—the Church still would like a dying individual to receive the Eucharist. Therefore the Church requires that under such circumstances, provided that an individual is reasonably sure the priest normally entrusted with administering viaticum would approve, any minister of Holy Communion—either ordinary or extraordinary—must administer viaticum.

To repeat, they *must* do this. Not only is it a right to bring viaticum to the dying but a serious obligation as well. Of course, the individual bringing viaticum in such a situation must subsequently notify the pastor of his or her action.

CHAPTER 12

Reception of Holy Communion

112. I hear a number of different things concerning who can and cannot receive Holy Communion. What does canon law say?

Canon 912 summarizes the Church's basic thinking when it comes to reception of Holy Communion: "Any baptized person who is not forbidden by law may and must be admitted to holy communion." This is a very simple canon but one that gives us theological and pastoral insight into how to interpret any other canon governing the reception of Holy Communion.

In short, the reception of Holy Communion is an essential right of all Catholics, and thus it may only be restricted or limited for a just reason. For the most part, such restrictions must be noted in canon law. In some of the questions that follow we will see under what circumstances the law forbids a baptized Catholic to receive Holy Communion.

Nevertheless, the presumption of law is that any individual who approaches the minister for Holy Communion is capable of receiving the sacrament. Therefore, in cases of doubt the minister must allow the individual to receive the Holy Eucharist.

Finally, the administration of the sacraments within the Catholic Church is generally limited to Catholics. Nevertheless, there are some exceptions that allow non-Catholics to receive the Eucharist from a Catholic minister, as well as Catholics to receive the Eucharist from a minister of a non-Catholic church in which the sacraments are valid.

113. I will be visiting a friend who wants me to attend Mass at her Russian Orthodox church. Can I go and receive Communion?

The broadest definition of *communion* is "a body of Christians sharing a common faith and discipline" (see *Merriam-Webster Dictionary*, online edition, 2004). Canon law adds to this definition by stating that "full communion" is marked by a common "profession of faith, the sacraments and ecclesiastical governance" (canon 205). As Catholics, we do not share full communion with other churches and Christian denominations. And though the Church must work to restore communion among all believers, it does not gloss over glaring differences.

As a rule, non-Catholics are not permitted to receive Holy Communion at a Catholic Mass, and Catholics are not to receive Communion in other churches (canon 844, paragraph 1). There are, however, exceptions.

If a Catholic is not able to approach a Catholic minister for the sacrament of Holy Communion, he or she may receive Communion from a minister "in whose Church [it is] valid" (canon 844, paragraph 2). In other words, there are a few branches of churches in the world that have validly ordained priests who, when celebrating the Lord's Supper, bring about the real presence of Christ in the Eucharist. The Orthodox Church is one such example. Other examples include the Old Catholic Church and the Polish National Church, but Protestant denominations are not among this group of churches.

114. Can my Russian Orthodox friend receive Communion in my Catholic church?

We do not share full ecclesiastical communion with the Orthodox Church. Though we share a common profession of faith and celebrate the same sacraments, we cannot agree on governance—namely, the role that the pope has in the universal Church. Nevertheless, because of our closeness on the first two matters (profession of faith and celebration of the same sacraments), we are in much closer communion with our Orthodox than with our Protestant brothers and sisters. Protestant traditions have moved in a very different direction in recent centuries.

As a consequence of our closeness to "eastern Churches not in full communion with the Catholic Church," Catholic ministers can give Holy Communion to members of these churches if "they spontaneously ask for [it] and are properly disposed" (canon 844, paragraph 3). This also applies to members of other churches that the Vatican judges to be in similar situations of communion. These are churches that make the same profession of faith and validly celebrate the sacraments—for example, some of the churches that broke away before the Council of Chalcedon in 451.

115. My pastor gave communion to a Lutheran woman in the hospital. How can this be?

This is a sensitive issue. As we explained in Question 114, Protestants are not to receive Holy Communion, as there is no ecclesiastical communion between the Protestant denominations and the Catholic Church. Nevertheless, there are exceptions to this rule.

In cases where a baptized non-Catholic person is facing death, "Catholic ministers may lawfully administer [the sacraments of penance, anointing of the sick, and Holy Communion]" to the individual. The sick person must be unable to approach his or her own minister. In addition, the person must "spontaneously" ask for these sacraments.

Furthermore, the individual must "demonstrate the Catholic faith in respect to these sacraments and [be] properly disposed" (canon 844, paragraph 4). This means the individual must understand that the Eucharist is the Body and Blood of Christ. Furthermore, the individual must be without grave sin for the reception of Communion, so he or she would usually make a confession beforehand.

There is another instance when a non-Catholic person can receive the sacrament of Holy Communion. If there is a "grave and pressing need," the diocesan bishop or a conference of bishops can permit it. This would be for a planned moment rather than a spontaneous decision, since prior consent needs to be acquired.

116. My daughter is preparing for her first Holy Communion. Does the canon list any prerequisites?

The first paragraph of canon 913 lists the following basic requirements for children making their first Holy Communion:

> For holy communion to be administered to children, it is required that they have sufficient knowledge and be accurately prepared, so that according to their capacity they understand what the mystery of Christ means, and are able to receive the Body of the Lord with faith and devotion.

This canon outlines three conditions that must be fulfilled before reception of first Holy Communion. First, the individual must have sufficient catechetical knowledge of the faith and must be adequately prepared to receive our Lord. Of course, both the knowledge and the preparation are to be kept at a level children can understand. In other words, children need not know theology as thoroughly as St. Thomas Aquinas.

The second requirement also takes into account the intellectual capacity of a child preparing for Holy Communion: The child must have a basic understanding of what the eucharistic mystery means.

Thirdly, children should be capable of receiving the Holy Eucharist with both faith and devotion. Again, the level of faith and devotion need only be basic. Given our fallen human nature, it is not expected that most children (let alone most adults) share the same level of faith and devotion as St. Francis of Assisi or St. Benedict!

117. Must a child in danger of death go through the entire process of catechesis outlined in the first paragraph of canon 913?

One of the present authors first faced this question with a family member who contracted a serious illness as a child. Although this person had not completed the catechetical prerequisites mentioned in the first paragraph of canon 913, she nevertheless would have been allowed to receive Holy Communion had her situation worsened. The second paragraph of canon 913 states, "The blessed Eucharist may, however, be administered to children in danger of death if they can distinguish the Body of Christ from ordinary food and receive communion with reverence."

We are all familiar with Christ's invitation in Matthew 19:14: "Let the little children come to me, and do not stop them." Taking Christ's invitation to heart, the Church does not wish to deny her children in danger of death the grace of the Blessed Eucharist. In such circumstances the Church waives most of the requirements a baptized child must fulfill before being admitted to first Holy Communion. He or she need only be capable of distinguishing the Holy Eucharist from ordinary bread and of receiving our Lord with reverence.

118. My son suffers from a severe form of autism, which makes catechesis next to impossible. Can he still make his first Holy Communion?

The Second Vatican Council upholds the Eucharist as the "source and summit of the Christian life." Thus the spiritual life of any Catholic would surely be incomplete if he or she were not permitted to receive the Eucharist. For this reason canon 912 states, "any baptized person not prohibited by law can and must be admitted to Holy Communion."

Canon law usually requires that a Latin Catholic be properly catechized prior to receiving his or her first Holy Communion. The law is silent concerning reception of the Holy Eucharist by the mentally and cognitively challenged. Therefore, in keeping with canon 17, we must answer this question by seeking "recourse to parallel places" in the law. A parallel place in this context is any canon that presents similar but not identical circumstances.

One such place is the second paragraph of canon 913, which allows children in danger of death to receive the Holy Eucharist "if they can distinguish the Body of Christ from ordinary food and receive communion with reverence." Your autistic child's situation can be said to be parallel to that of the dying child in that both are unable to receive the necessary catechesis. So, applying the second paragraph of canon 913 to your child, you need to discern if he or she "can distinguish the Body of Christ from ordinary food and receive communion with reverence."

119. In answering the two previous questions, you mentioned that a child in danger of death or a child who suffers from mental or cognitive disability may receive the Holy Eucharist if he or she can distinguish between a consecrated Host and ordinary bread. Must the capacity to do so be verbal?

No, the capacity to distinguish need not necessarily be verbal. Such a requirement would exclude children whose verbal incapacity is part of their extraordinary medical condition.

Thus when it comes to children in danger of death, as well as children who are mentally or cognitively challenged, the capacity to distinguish between the Eucharist and ordinary food may also be demonstrated in some other way that is more suited to their particular condition.

For example, an autistic child may demonstrate this capacity through reverential silence or some other pious gesture. We refer you to the United States Catholic Bishops' *Guidelines for Celebration of the Sacraments with Persons with Disabilities*, no. 20. Invoking the ancient canonical principle that "favors are to be multiplied and burdens restricted," the U.S. Bishops remind us,

> Cases of doubt should be resolved in favor of the right of the baptized person to receive the Sacrament. The existence of a disability is not considered in and of itself as disqualifying a person from receiving the Eucharist.

120. Whose duty is it to ensure that children are properly prepared for their first Holy Communion?

Canon 914 answers:

> It is primarily the duty of parents and of those who take their place, as it is the duty of the parish priest, to ensure that chil-

dren who have reached the use of reason are properly prepared and, having made their sacramental confession, are nourished by this divine food as soon as possible. It is also the duty of the parish priest to see that children who have not reached the use of reason, or whom he has judged to be insufficiently disposed, do not come to holy communion.

This canon is fairly self-explanatory, although many Catholics are not aware of its contents. First of all, it is the primary duty of parents to ensure that their children are properly prepared for first Holy Communion. Parents must not abdicate this obligation to their children's religious education teachers. The duty—not just the right but the *duty*—is first and foremost that of the parents.

Secondly, the parish priest shares in this duty to make sure a child is properly prepared to receive Holy Communion. If this is not possible within a given time frame, then the pastor also has the duty to withhold first Holy Communion until the child is ready.

121. I notice that canon 914 lists the making of a sacramental confession as a prerequisite to receiving first Holy Communion. Since most seven-year-olds have not obtained the sufficient use of reason to commit a mortal sin, why should they be compelled to make a sacramental confession prior to receiving their first Holy Communion?

Canon 914's requirement of a sacramental confession before first Communion is often ignored in our day. As you aptly point out, many pastors and catechists argue that a young child is incapable of committing a mortal sin.

Father William Woestman, a respected professor of canon law, often replied to these arguments as follows: "As a priest, the Church recommends that I go to confession often. However, the Church most certainly does not expect me to commit mortal sins on a regular basis."

Even if a child has not committed a mortal sin during his or her brief lifetime, he or she should still be given the opportunity to make a sacramental confession prior to receiving first Holy Communion. This helps develop in children the good habit of regular and sincere confession and reverence for the Eucharist.

122. Can a Catholic be forbidden to receive Holy Communion?

Canon 915 is clear: Those upon whom the penalty of excommunication or interdict has been imposed or declared, and others who obstinately persist in manifest grave sin, are not to be admitted to holy communion.

As already mentioned, Catholics who approach Holy Communion have the right to receive our Lord, unless otherwise stated in the law. Here is one of the exceptions stated within canon law.

When the Church excommunicates or places under interdict an individual, she does so not with the intention of punishing the individual. Rather, she intends to help the individual repent of whatever crime led to the penalty. Thus the Church bars the individual from receiving Holy Communion in order to force the individual to reflect upon how his or her crime wounded Christ's Mystical Body. Once the individual repents and has the penalty lifted, he or she may be readmitted to Holy Communion.

Similarly, the Church must refuse Communion to those who obstinately persist in mortal sin—again, with the intention of helping these individuals come to repentance. Notice that the persistence must also be obstinate—that is, the individual must be forewarned by the Church but choose to continue the mortally sinful situation anyway.

One example of such behavior would be a Catholic's attempt to contract marriage outside of the Church without the Church's permission. The politician who intentionally supports laws facilitating and promoting abortion presents another example. Such individuals have the right to be readmitted to Holy Communion once they repent of their sinful situation.

123. If there is no opportunity to make a sacramental confession beforehand, can I still receive Holy Communion?

Canon 916 addresses this question:

> Anyone who is conscious of grave sin may not celebrate Mass or receive the Body of the Lord without previously having been to sacramental confession, unless there is a grave reason and there is no opportunity to confess; in this case the person is to remember the obligation to make an act of perfect contrition, which includes the resolve to go to confession as soon as possible.

Most Catholics know they should not receive Holy Communion if they have unconfessed grave sin on their conscience. Yet this canon contains an exception. If a serious reason prevents one from going to sacramental confession, and there is no foreseeable opportunity in the future to do so, then one may still receive Holy Communion provided one meets the following two conditions: First, one must make as perfect an act of contrition as possible—that is, show remorse for having offended God through one's mortal sins. Second, one must be personally resolved to receive the sacrament of confession as soon as possible.

For instance, some small communities in northern Ontario can only be reached by bush plane. Quite often these communities are too small to have a priest stationed with them permanently. During the Christmas and Easter seasons, if a priest is not available, the diocesan bishop will send a deacon, a religious brother, or a religious sister to lead the community in a Communion service. Such a scenario allows a member of the community to receive Holy Communion after making as perfect an act of contrition as possible.

124. I often attend Mass twice on a given weekday—once in the morning with my elderly mother and once in the evening with my husband and children. Am I permitted to receive Holy Communion only once a day, or can I receive at both Masses?

As some readers may remember, prior to the Second Vatican Council it was only permissible for the faithful to receive Holy Communion once a day. Part of the reason for this was to curb a certain abuse whereby some faithful attempted to receive the Eucharist as many times a day as possible. While the Holy Eucharist is certainly supernatural, our Lord should never become the object of superstition.

The 1983 *Code of Canon Law* takes a much more generous position toward receiving Holy Communion more than once a day. Canon 917 states,

> One who has received the blessed Eucharist may receive it again on the same day only within a eucharistic celebration in which that person participates, without prejudice to the provision of canon 921, paragraph 2.

Ignoring the reference to canon 921 for the moment—which deals with viaticum—canon law now permits Catholics to receive Holy Communion twice a day. Owing to an ambiguity in the original Latin text, however, canonists were initially unsure how to interpret this canon. Some felt the canon limited reception of Holy Communion to twice a day, while others understood the Latin text to mean any number of subsequent opportunities to receive the Holy Eucharist in a given day.

The Pontifical Council for Legislative Texts subsequently clarified that canon 917 applies only to a second opportunity to receive Holy Communion in a given day. The interpretation of this Pontifical Council is both authoritative and binding. Additionally, the canon clearly states that any second opportunity to receive Holy Communion in a given day must take place in the context of the Mass. Viaticum provides the only exception, since the Church wishes for one to receive the Holy Eucharist whenever a serious danger of death presents itself.

125. Are Catholics still required to fast before receiving Holy Communion, or has the Church done away with this requirement?

The first paragraph of canon 919 states, "Whoever is to receive the blessed Eucharist is to abstain for at least one hour before holy communion from all food and drink, with the sole exception of water and medicine." Thus the eucharistic fast, while greatly reduced since the Second Vatican Council, still stands.

This canon is notable for several reasons. First of all, the minimal length of the eucharistic fast is "one hour before holy communion" and not one hour before the beginning of the Mass. This usually means that one can safely feed one's children prior to frequenting longer liturgies such as the Mass of Holy Chrism and even some Sunday liturgies.

Secondly, there are a number of exceptions to the eucharistic fast. The first paragraph of canon 919 states two of these—namely, medicine and water. Although the eucharistic fast symbolizes the precedence of food for the soul over food for the body, the Church nevertheless does not wish anyone to be excluded from receiving our Lord due to a medical necessity. Therefore, canon law permits Catholics to take medicine and water prior to receiving Holy Communion.

126. You mentioned medicine and water as exceptions to the Eucharistic fast, but what if someone requires food due to age, illness, or pregnancy?

The third paragraph of canon 919 provides the answer to this question: The elderly and those who are suffering from some illness, as well as those who care for them, may receive the blessed Eucharist even if within the preceding hour they have consumed something.

Again, the purpose of the eucharistic fast is not to prohibit Catholics from receiving Holy Communion because of circumstances beyond their control. Thus those who suffer from some illness, disability, or injury are allowed to consume food and drink before going to Holy Communion if it is necessary for them to do so. The same applies to those who care for these individuals, as the Church recognizes that caregivers require their strength as well.

The Church does not look upon pregnancy as an illness but as one of the many blessings of marriage. Nevertheless, most canonists agree that pregnant women are implicitly included in the exceptions to the eucharistic fast. After all, Catholic mothers are no different from other mothers when it comes to the physical and dietary demands of pregnancy. Or as canonists often joke when discussing this issue, "As a pro-life Church we recognize that a pregnant mother is eating for her baby, who is not bound to the Church's laws of fast and abstinence."

127. How often does the Church require Catholics to receive the Holy Eucharist?

According to the first paragraph of canon 920, "Once admitted to the blessed Eucharist, each of the faithful is obliged to receive holy communion at least once a year." The second paragraph of this canon continues: "This precept must be fulfilled during paschal time, unless for a good reason it is fulfilled at another time during the year."

Most Catholics refer to the contents of this canon as "our Easter duty." Basically, we should receive the Holy Eucharist at least once a year, after a sacramental confession. The law prefers that our Easter duty be fulfilled during the Easter season. In the United States of America, this means from the First Sunday of Lent up until Trinity Sunday. In most of the rest of the world, this means from Palm (Passion) Sunday through Pentecost. Nevertheless, it can be fulfilled outside of the Easter season for a good reason. A sacrilegious Communion does not fulfill this obligation.

The purpose of this law is to encourage Catholics not to neglect receiving the sacraments. Additionally, the annual reception of the Eucharist is merely the Church's minimal requirement. With few exceptions, every modern pope from St. Pius X to John Paul II has encouraged Catholics to receive our Lord daily whenever possible.

128. What is viaticum, and when should I receive it?

According to the first paragraph of canon 921, "Christ's faithful who are in danger of death, from whatever cause, are to be strengthened by holy communion as Viaticum." In short, the Church does not wish her children to depart from this life without Christ's accompaniment. Therefore, insofar as we are capable when the danger of death threatens, we are to be strengthened through our Lord's real presence. Thus viaticum is Holy Communion administered to one in danger of death.

"Even if they have already received holy communion that same day," the second paragraph of canon 921 continues, "it is nevertheless strongly suggested that in danger of death they should communicate again." As mentioned in response to Question 125, ordinarily one should receive Holy Communion only within the context of the Mass when receiving more than once in a given day. The purpose of this second paragraph is to clarify the reception of viaticum as an exception to this rule. When the danger of death presents itself, one should seek viaticum whether or not one previously received Holy Communion during the day.

Finally, one should seek viaticum more than once when the danger of death is prolonged. The only requirement is that viaticum be administered on separate days. This is clear from the third paragraph of canon 921: "While the danger of death persists, it is recommended that holy communion be administered a number of times, but on separate days."

129. I am a Latin Catholic. Does the Church permit me to receive Holy Communion in an Eastern Catholic church?

According to canon 923, "Christ's faithful may participate in the eucharistic Sacrifice and receive holy communion in any Catholic rite, without prejudice to the provisions of canon 844."

Especially since the Second Vatican Council, the Church has focused both on the Eucharist and the universal nature of the Church. Canon 923 brings both together. We may participate, receive our Lord, and fulfill our various obligations within any Catholic rite of Mass approved by the Church. Therefore, Latin

Catholics fulfill their Sunday obligation when visiting an Eastern Catholic church for Sunday Mass. Because the *Code of Canons of the Eastern Churches* contains a similar canon, the same principle applies to Eastern Catholics who visit Latin Catholic churches.

This canon adds "without prejudice to the provisions of canon 844." This canon, as you may remember from Questions 114 and 115, obliges Catholics not to receive the sacraments outside of the Catholic Church unless certain exceptional circumstances apply. For example, if no Catholic priest was around and a Catholic found himself in danger of death, under canon 844 he could seek viaticum from the local Greek Orthodox priest. These exceptional circumstances do not need to be present when considering Communion in an Eastern Catholic church.

CHAPTER 13

Confession and Anointing of the Sick

130. According to canon law, what is the purpose of the sacrament of confession?

Canon 959 summarizes the purpose of this sacrament as follows: In the sacrament of penance the faithful who confess their sins to a lawful minister, are sorry for those sins and have a purpose of amendment, receive from God, through the absolution given by that minister, forgiveness of sins they have committed after baptism, and at the same time they are reconciled with the Church, which by sinning they wounded.

In short, the purpose of the sacrament of confession is twofold. First, one receives absolution—that is, Christ's forgiveness—from one's sins committed after baptism. Secondly, one is reconciled to Christ and his Church.

The canon outlines several steps that must be taken prior to receiving absolution in the sacrament. First, the penitent must approach a lawful minister of the sacrament—namely, a bishop or a priest with faculties from the priest's diocesan bishop or religious superior. Secondly, the penitent must be sorry for his or her sins.

Thirdly, the penitent must possess a firm purpose of amendment. This means the penitent should be personally resolved not to sin again. Of course, given our fallen human nature, most of us will sin again, but we are to be firmly resolved at the time of our confession to sin no more. Finally, the penitent must confess all serious sin—that is, mortal sin—on his or her conscience.

A penitent making a first confession must confess all mortal sins committed since baptism. In the cases of subsequent confessions, a penitent need only confess all serious sin not previously confessed.

131. What is the ordinary means of administering the sacrament of confession?

According to canon 960, "individual and integral confession and absolution constitute the sole ordinary means by which a member of the faithful who is conscious of grave sin is reconciled with God and with the Church."

The term *individual* simply refers to the fact that the penitent approaches the priest or bishop for a one-on-one encounter with the sacrament. Depending upon the circumstances, this may take place in an old-fashioned confessional, a modern reconciliation room, or any other venue that respects the privacy of priest and penitent. In keeping with canon 964, however, this should be in a church or oratory.

The word *integral* refers to the fact that the penitent must confess all previously unconfessed mortal sins, to the best of his or her recollection.

While the Church also recognizes the validity of general absolution in certain instances, this is considered an extraordinary means of receiving the sacrament. Ordinarily one must seek absolution through individual and integral confession.

132. Does general absolution remove one's obligation to confess mortal sins privately?

Canon 962, paragraph 1, states:

> For a member of Christ's faithful to benefit validly from a sacramental absolution given to a number of people simultaneously, it is required not only that he or she be properly disposed, but also that he or she be at the same time personally resolved to confess in due time each of the grave sins which cannot for the moment be confessed.

In order to be validly absolved from one's sins in general absolution, one must have contrition for one's sins along with a firm purpose of amendment. This is what being "properly disposed" refers to. These are the same conditions that apply to any private confession.

Moreover, one must be resolved to confess one's mortal sins privately in due time. The expression *in due time* is not defined in canon law.

One should note from canon 962 that the intention of the penitent at the time of the general absolution determines whether or not he or she validly receives general absolution. A valid general absolution does not become invalid if one fails to follow through on one's intention to confess privately. This is because the valid administration of a sacrament can never be based upon the fulfillment of a future condition. What is important is the present resolve of the penitent.

133. When giving general absolution, is the priest required to instruct the faithful about their obligation to privately confess all mortal sins? Is this a matter of lawfulness or validity?

The second paragraph of canon 962 states:

> Christ's faithful are to be instructed about [the requirement to privately confess all mortal sin in due time], as far as possible even on the occasion of general absolution being received. An exhortation that each person should make an act of contrition is to precede a general absolution, even in the case of danger of death if there is time.

In answer to the first question, the minister should ensure that the faithful in attendance are adequately instructed. They should be made aware, prior to receiving general absolution, of their obligation to confess all mortal sins in due time.

Keep in mind that the requirement that the penitent be resolved to confess his or her mortal sins in due time is for validity. Nevertheless, the obligation to instruct the faithful is for lawfulness only. Therefore, if the minister of general absolution forgets to instruct the faithful, the absolution received is still valid provided that the faithful are resolved to confess privately their mortal sins in due time.

If possible, the minister of the sacrament should also lead the faithful in an act of contrition prior to administering general absolution.

134. Who can hear my confession and give me absolution in a necessity?

"In an urgent necessity," the second paragraph of canon 986 states, "every confessor is bound to hear the confessions of Christ's faithful, and in danger of death every priest is so obliged." This canon distinguishes between a priest and a confessor. The former is a validly ordained priest or bishop, while the latter is a validly ordained priest or bishop with faculties from his competent ecclesiastical superior to hear confessions.

In an urgent necessity, every confessor is bound to hear confessions. The canon deliberately avoids defining *urgent necessity,* leaving it up to the good judgment of the individual confessor. The same applies to the expression *in danger of death.*

One should note that the law obliges *every* validly ordained priest and bishop to hear confessions when the danger of death presents itself. This even includes priests who have been laicized, suspended, or excommunicated. One may even approach a validly ordained non-Catholic priest at such a time. For instance, if no Catholic priest is available, one may call upon an Eastern Orthodox priest or a priest of the Polish National Catholic Church within the vicinity.

135. My deaf sister recently moved in with our family. None of the priests in our town know sign language. Would accompanying her into the confessional violate the seal of confession?

Not if your purpose in accompanying her is to serve as translator between her and the priest. Canon 990 clearly states, "No one is forbidden to confess through an interpreter, provided however that abuse and scandal are avoided, and without prejudice to the provision of canon 983, paragraph 2."

The second paragraph of canon 983 simply binds the translator or interpreter to observe the inviolability of the seal of confession. In other words, like the priest, a translator or interpreter may not divulge the contents of the confession. The text of this canon is "An interpreter, if there is one, is also obliged to observe this secret, as are all others who in any way whatever have come to a knowledge of sins from a confession."

136. My fiancée is a devout Ukrainian Catholic. As a Latin Catholic, can I approach her Ukrainian Catholic pastor for confession?

Absolutely. This is in keeping with canon 991: "All Christ's faithful are free to confess their sins to lawfully approved confessors of their own choice, even to one of another rite."

The Second Vatican Council deepened the Church's under-standing of communion among Catholics of different liturgical and patrimonial backgrounds—for example, Eastern Catholics. Catholics are no longer bound to receive the sacraments from priests of their own liturgical background.

Nor are Catholics still required to make their Easter confession to their local pastor. Rather, a Catholic may approach any confessor for the sacrament of confession. As previously mentioned, a confessor is a Catholic priest or bishop who possesses from his lawful ecclesiastical superior the faculty to hear confessions. A confessor may be of the Latin Catholic Church, the Maronite Catholic Church, the Melkite Catholic Church, or any of the other Eastern Catholic Churches.

137. Our pastor often administers the sacrament of anointing of the sick to my grandmother, despite the fact that she is not dying. Is this lawful?

Yes, this is a lawful and good practice.

Too often Catholics misunderstand the sacrament of anointing of the sick. Although the Church encourages those on their deathbed to receive this sacrament, it is not exclusively the sacra-ment of the dying. The first paragraph of canon 1004 clarifies this: "The anointing of the sick can be administered to any member of the faithful who, having reached the use of reason, begins to be in danger by reason of illness or old age."

The canon presents the requirements for receiving this sacrament:

- One must be a Catholic.
- One must have attained the use of reason, which is generally presumed after completing one's seventh year of age.
- One must be in some sort of danger due to illness or old age.

Notice that the canon does not use the expression *danger of death*. This is because the purpose of this sacrament is to strengthen those who are "dangerously ill" (canon 998) and not only those who are deathly ill. The danger spoken of in the canon is any serious danger to one's health.

138. Our four-year-old son was recently diagnosed with leukemia. Can he receive the sacrament of anointing of the sick despite the fact that he has not reached the age of reason?

When it comes to the reception of this sacrament, canon 1004 specifies those who have "reached the *use* of reason" and not necessarily those who have obtained "the *age* of reason" (emphasis ours). While canon law sets the age of reason at the completion of one's seventh year, which in canonical time is the day after one's seventh birthday, this is simply the age by which canon law presumes an individual has obtained the use of reason.

Nevertheless, canonists recognize that attaining the use of reason does not suddenly happen the night of one's seventh birthday. Rather, it is a process that begins at birth and progresses through infancy and childhood. Additionally, different children develop their reasoning faculties at different rates. Therefore, it is likely that a four-year-old has attained at least the partial use of reason.

Having anticipated the difficult situation in which you find yourselves, canon 1005 offers the following pastoral solution: "If there is any doubt as to whether the sick person has reached the use of reason, or is dangerously ill, or is dead, this sacrament is to be administered."

139. Can the sacrament of anointing of the sick be repeated? If so, can it be repeated several times or only once?

In response to the above questions, the sacrament may be repeated as many times as necessary. This is clear from the second paragraph of canon 1004: "This sacrament can be repeated if the sick person, having recovered, again becomes seriously ill or if, in the same illness, the danger becomes more serious."

The sacrament may be repeated if one's illness returns after an interlude of recovery. For example, suppose an individual was diagnosed with cancer. Prior to undergoing radiation treatment, the individual sought comfort in the sacrament of anointing of the sick. As the radiation treatment progressed, the cancer regressed into remission. Should the cancer ever return, the individual may again seek spiritual comfort in the sacrament of anointing of the sick.

Secondly, the sacrament may be repeated if one's illness worsens. For instance, testing positive for HIV often forces an individual to confront his or her mortality. For most people the transition from HIV to AIDS happens over time, as one's immune system slowly breaks down. One may receive the sacrament of anointing of the sick at each stage of the illness.

CHAPTER 14

Marriage and Annulment

140. How does canon law define marriage?

The first paragraph of canon 1055 defines marriage:

> The marriage covenant, by which a man and a woman establish between themselves a partnership of their whole life, and which of its own very nature is ordered to the well-being of the spouses and to the procreation and upbringing of children, has, between the baptized, been raised by Christ the Lord to the dignity of a sacrament.

To begin, marriage is a covenant. In other words, it is a pact through which the spouses promise to assist one another toward a common purpose. This marital covenant is exclusive to one man and one woman. The couple establishes a partnership between themselves for the whole of life—that is, until one spouse dies. This is known as *permanence* or *indissolubility*.

By its very nature, marriage is ordered toward the good of the spouses. Husband and wife promise to assist and support each other in all their physical, emotional, material, and spiritual needs.

Marriage is also ordered toward the procreation and upbringing of children. The couple must be open to conceiving children and must agree to work together to raise any child born or adopted into the marriage.

Finally, when both parties are baptized, the marriage is a sacrament.

141. What is the difference between a sacramental marriage and a natural marriage?

We can take the above description from canon 1055 as the definition of natural marriage. This is what is common to all marriages. When both the husband and the wife are baptized Christians, this natural marriage takes on the additional element of sacramentality.

As a sacrament, a marriage between two baptized persons is a visible sign of God's love in the world. The couple finds in their relationship a source of God's grace, and through their partnership they assist one another in coming closer to God.

The very fact that both husband and wife are baptized makes their marriage a sacrament. This is also true of a marriage between two baptized Protestants before a justice of the peace.

Additionally, a natural marriage will automatically become a sacramental marriage when both parties are baptized.

142. What is the canonical form of marriage?

For Latin Catholics the canonical form of marriage is the exchange of matrimonial consent (the wedding vows) before a qualified witness and two witnesses. The qualified witness is a bishop, a priest, a deacon, or in certain circumstances some other appointed minister. The qualified witness must possess delegation by law from the diocesan bishop or from the proper pastor of that parish. The two witnesses may be any two individuals chosen by the people.

For Eastern Catholics the qualified witness must be either the diocesan bishop or a priest with delegation. This is because within Eastern Catholic theology, the blessing of the priest brings the marriage into being.

A Latin Catholic may enter into marriage with a non-Catholic before a non-Catholic minister, provided a dispensation (relaxation of the law) from canonical form is granted by the competent Church authority. This kind of dispensation is the exception.

143. My parish charges $500 for the celebration of a wedding. This is an outrageous fee. Can the pastor do this?

The spiritual riches of the Church cannot be used for profit making. The law states that when celebrating a sacrament, a bishop, priest, or deacon may not ask for anything beyond the offerings that are determined by the bishops of the region (canon 848 and canon 1264).

There was a time when a diocesan priest had to rely solely on offerings for support. For instance, he would collect a stipend whenever he offered a Mass for an individual. In modern times a salary is administered by the diocese to compensate priests. Nevertheless, stipends still exist.

The bishops of a region are to agree on acceptable stipend amounts for the sacraments or other religious acts, including the sacrament of marriage. A parish must receive permission to charge more than the stipend amount set by the bishop. You can inquire about the stipend amount by calling the diocesan chancery.

The cost of celebrating a sacrament actually can cost more than the stipend provides. For instance, a Saturday afternoon wedding on a cold winter's day could cost a parish a sizeable amount in heating, janitorial, and snow removal costs. In such a case the diocese may permit an increase to the stipend level, but this increase goes not into the priest's pocket but into the parish budget.

144. I want to get married in a historical Catholic church on the other side of town, but the pastor has refused since I do not reside in the area. Can he do this?

A pastor is obliged to celebrate marriage for his parishioners only. In other words, a person cannot "church shop." Canon law states that "marriages are to be celebrated in the parish in which either of the contracting parties has a domicile or a quasi-domicile or a month's residence" (canon 1115).

As indicated in the answer to Question 48 in Chapter 6, every Catholic in the world belongs to the parish in which he or she resides. Even though a Catholic may register in a parish, he or she does not have a right to receive the sacraments in that parish.

The distinction that this canon makes between "domicile" and "quasi-domicile" is simpler than it sounds. *Domicile* refers to living in a location for at least five years or, having moved to a place, intending to stay there indefinitely. *Quasi-domicile* refers to living in a place for at least three months. Finally, the law provides another qualifying period of time, "one-month residence."

As frustrating as it sounds, the pastor in this historical parish has every right to say no to a request from one who is not a parishioner. You'd better try your own parish.

145. What is the annulment process?

Canon 1060 states, "Marriage enjoys the favor of the law. Consequently, in doubt the validity of a marriage must be upheld until the contrary is proven."

Provided that each spouse was free to marry—meaning that each spouse was of canonical age and was not bound by previous religious vows or promises—the Church automatically assumes that a marriage is indeed a valid marriage. This is what canon law means when it states that "marriage enjoys the favor of the law." Subsequently, a divorced person is not free to attempt another marriage within the Catholic Church so long as the spouse from the previous marriage is still living.

The annulment process is a judicial process in which the Church examines the presumption of validity of a particular marriage. The Church investigates the history of the couple's relationship to see if there were any problems that prevented the marriage from coming together at its inception. If sufficient evidence can be proven with moral certitude, then the presumption of validity may be overturned. The Church then issues a declaration of nullity or an annulment, and the individuals may be declared free to marry.

146. What are some of the reasons for granting an annulment?

The Code of Canon Law lists several grounds upon which a marriage can be declared invalid. In North America the two most common grounds concern the psychological maturity of either person at the time of the wedding and the intention with which a person attempts marriage.

Canonists refer to the first ground as "a grave lack of discretion of judgment." The second paragraph of canon 1095 outlines this ground. In investigating this ground, the tribunal examines the psychological maturity and the day-to-day judgment of the individual around the time of the wedding. How well was the individual prepared for marriage? How well did the person know his or her future spouse? Did he or she freely choose to marry, or was the wedding a reaction to strong internal pressure? For example, many couples rush into marriage after discovering a premarital pregnancy. The other ground commonly used by North American tribunals is called "simulation." Outlined in the second paragraph of canon 1101, simulation concerns the intention of the individual at the time of the wedding. Simulation may be total—that is, the individual goes through the motions of the wedding but truly does not wish to marry. More commonly, simulation is partial: The individual excludes something essential to marriage, such as fidelity to the spouse or openness to having children.

Several other grounds are available to canonists. Therefore, you should not try to discern potential grounds by yourself when considering the possibility of an annulment. Rather, check with your parish priest or diocesan marriage tribunal.

147. Are annulments Catholic divorces?

No. A Catholic annulment, also known as a declaration of nullity or a declaration of invalidity, is a statement of fact by the Catholic Church. After carefully examining the couple's broken relationship, the Church states that a valid marriage, as the Church defines marriage, never existed.

Annulment is not "Catholic divorce" because divorce ends a marriage that once existed. Rather, a declaration of nullity or annulment maintains that from the very beginning, something necessary to marriage was lacking in the relationship.

Of course, the Church recognizes that the couple initially had some form of relationship. In countries where civil authorities also regulate marriage, the Church acknowledges that the relationship was once recognized as a marriage by civil law. If an invalid marriage was attempted in good faith by at least one of the spouses, the Church then refers to it as a "putative marriage."

148. Why do I need an annulment if I am not Catholic?

Oftentimes a divorced non-Catholic seeking to marry a Catholic is required to go through the annulment process first. This seems strange to most non-Catholics, especially if neither spouse from the first marriage was baptized or received into the Catholic Church. Nevertheless, the Catholic Church presumes the validity of any marriage between two people who are free to marry. Therefore, if two non-Catholics marry in a civil or religious ceremony that is recognized by the state, then the Catholic Church must also assume the validity of the marriage.

The Catholic Church believes her teaching concerning the indissolubility of marriage to be part of God's natural law. Therefore this teaching binds all people, regardless of whether or not they are Catholic.

The Church cannot permit a Catholic to marry someone who is bound by a previous marriage.

So if a divorced non-Catholic wishes to marry a Catholic, then the Catholic Church must investigate the previous marriage to see if the presumption of validity may be overturned. Only if the previous marriage is null can the non-Catholic contract a marriage with a Catholic.

149. Are there any other options for ending a marriage, besides petitioning for a declaration of nullity?

Yes. Under certain circumstances, a marriage may be dissolved in favor of a new marriage. A dissolution is different from the annulment process in that it recognizes the existence of the first marriage, whereas a declaration of nullity establishes that the first marriage never existed. A dissolution is of limited applicability, since a sacramental marriage cannot be dissolved once it has been consummated.

That being said, if one of the spouses was not baptized during the first marriage, and the lack of baptism can be proven, then the marriage was not a sacrament. Then a "privilege of the faith" case can be sent to the Holy See. If both parties were baptized, but the marriage was never consummated, then the case may be sent to the Holy See as a "Petrine privilege."

In either case the individual petitioning for the dissolution cannot have been the cause of the marital breakdown. If the Holy See approves, the non-sacramental marriage may be dissolved in favor of a sacramental marriage.

In another common scenario, neither of the spouses was baptized prior to the wedding, and now one of the spouses wishes to be baptized and marry a Catholic. Provided one can prove that neither spouse of the first marriage was baptized, a "Pauline privilege" is possible. In this situation, the diocesan bishop allows the non-sacramental partnership to be dissolved in favor of the new marriage. Of course, the spouse desiring baptism must be baptized before entering into the new marriage.

150. Are my children considered illegitimate if I obtain an annulment?

Church law clearly states that children born within a marriage that was entered into "in good faith" are not to be considered illegitimate (canon 1137). *In good faith* means that at the time of the wedding one or both people truly believed that they were establishing a marriage. This holds true even if the marriage, at a later date, is declared null (that is, invalid according to Church law).

Church law has not completely dropped reference to the legitimacy of children. Children born to single parent families or in a civil union that is not recognized by Church law are regarded as illegitimate. It should be noted that Church law does not create any obstacle for a child born outside of marriage. Though our Western culture has used the term *illegitimate* in a derogatory way, these children have a right to the sacraments, catechesis, and all the respect due children of God.

Have Additional Questions?

We hope you enjoyed reading this book as much as we enjoyed writing it. In reviewing the manuscript, we decided not to write a conclusion. We know from experience that people will always have more canon law questions. So a concluding chapter seemed a little out of place.

Certainly the editorial staff of Servant had more questions, as did those who reviewed the manuscript prior to publication. We anticipate that you the reader have some additional questions about canon law as well.

Please e-mail your canon law questions to www.surprisedby canonlaw.com. If you do not have Internet access, you may also send your questions via postal mail to:

Canon Law Questions
c/o Book Dept.
St. Anthony Messenger Press
28 W. Liberty St.
Cincinnati, OH 45202

Given the number of questions we receive each week, we unfortunately cannot answer every question that comes our way (at least not without the risk that our wives would petition the local tribunal for an annulment). Nevertheless, we promise to read every question; and should our Lord bless us with the opportunity to write another book, we will answer the more common questions you raise.

INDEX

Abortion
    Excommunication and, 9
Annulment
    Process of, 116
    Reasons for, 116-117
    As Catholic divorce, 117
    For non-Catholics,118
    Legitimacy of children and, 119
Anointing of the sick, sacrament of,
        109-110
    For children, 110-111
    Repetition of, 111
Apostasy, 49
Archbishop, role of, 36
Autism, and reception of
        sacraments, 75, 95-96

Baptism, sacrament of
    As prerequisite for communion
        with church, 12
    Necessary for church
        membership, 13
    Infant, 63-64-69
    Consent, 64-65
    Catechetical formation prior to,
        65
    And the mentally challenged,
        65-66
    And saints' names, 66
    Appropriate time for, 66-67
    At home, 67-68
    Godparents and, 68
Bible, translations of, 60

Bishop
    Auxiliary, 34-35
    Title of, 33-4

Canon, 4
Canon law
    Importance of, 1, 3
    Definition of, 3
Canonists (see canon lawyers)
Canon lawyers, 3
Catechism of the Catholic Church, 14-15
Charismatic Renewal, 17
Code of Canon Law
    On baptism, 63
    Books of, 5-6
    Need for, 4
    Origin of, 4
    Rights under, 19-20
    And Sacred Scripture, 60
    Those governed by, 6
Cardinal, title of, 33-34
Catholics
    Use of term, 29
    Responsibilities of, 50-51
Catholic schools, 56
    Religious curriculum in, 57
    Teachers in, 57-58
    Of higher education, 58
Censors 59-60
Chancellor, role of, 39-40
Clergy
    Rights and obligations of, 21-27
    Assignment of, 23

Worldliness and, 24
Education of, 24
Preparation for ordination, 22
Religious orders and, 23
Diocesan, 23, 25
Political office, and, 24
Removal of, 26-27
Retirement of, 31
Complaints of, 40
Role in celebrating Mass, 81, 87
Standing of, 82-83
Frequency of Mass for, 84-86
Conference of Catholic Bishops, 37
Communion (with Roman Catholic
    Church)
Definition of, as applied to other
    churches, 11-12
Need for celebration of
    sacraments, 12
Confession, sacrament of
As prerequisite for Communion,
    97, 99
Purpose of, 105
General absolution and, 106-108
Urgent necessity and, 108
Through a translator, 108-109
Of the deaf, 108-109
Confirmation, sacrament of, 68, 71
In Eastern Catholic churches, 71
Oil used in, 72
Celebration of, 73
Ordinary ministers of, 73-74
Minimum age for, 74-75
Autism and, 75
And special needs children, 75-76
Qualifications of sponsors, 76

Cursillo Movement, 16
Custom, 7, 10

Deacons, permanent, 22-23
Declaration of nullity (see
    annulment)
Dioceses
    Origin of, 33
    Function of, 33
    Management of, 34-36, 38-39
Divine Liturgy (see Mass)

Eastern Catholicism, 11-12, 13-14,
    71, 103-104
Ecclesiastical law, 5
Ecumenical law, 5
Ecumenical work, 11
Eucharist, sacrament of (see also
    Mass), 13
Reverence toward, 80
    Celebration of 80-81, 87
    Viaticum, 88-89, 102-103
    Reception of, 91, 98
    In Eastern Catholic Church,
        103-104
    By Non-Catholics, 91-93
    By Catholics in non-Catholic
        Church, 92
    Frequency of, 99-100, 102
Education, Church's role in, 52-53,
    55, 56
Excommunication, in cases of
    abortion, 9
Ex corde ecclesiae, 58
Extraordinary ministers of
    Communion, 18, 87

Fasting, 100-102
Franciscans, 23

General norms (see norms, general)
Godparents, 68-70

Heresy, 48-49
Homilies, given by layperson, 52

Imprimatur, 60

Laicization, 27
Laity, obligations of, 18
Lefebvre, Archbishop, 7-8
Licentiate, 3
Licit, definition of, 7
Liturgical law, 5

Magisterium, 32
Marriage, sacrament of
    Canonical form, 114
    Choice of church for, 115-116
    Fees for, 114-115
    Options for ending, 118-119
    Right of non-parishioners to, 15
    Sacramental vs. natural, 113-114
Mass, 18
    As communal celebration, 81-82
    Necessity of priest for, 82-83
    Changing words of, 83
    Offered for non-Catholics, 84
    Frequency of, for clergy, 84-85
    Celebration of, alone, 86-87
Metropolitan bishops (*see*
    archbishops)

Norms, general, 6-7

Opus Dei, 23
Orthodox Church, 11-12

Parishes
    Attendance, 41
    Councils, 44-45
    Finances, 45
    Pastors, 41-42
Pastors, 42-43
    Removal of, 46
    Vacation of, 44
Petrine privilege, 119
Politics, church's role in, 47
Pontifical universities, 59
Pope
    Authority of, 29
    Infallibility of, 47-48
    Origin of role, 29
    Resignation of, 30
Profession of faith, necessary for
    communion, 12
Protestantism, 12

RCIA, 13
Reputation, right to, 17
Retirement of clergy, 31
Right of association, 15-16
Rights, canonical, 11
    To sacraments, 14-15
    To reputation, 17
Roman Catholic Church,
    membership in, 12-13

Sacramental law, 5
Sacraments (see also individual
    sacraments)
    Right to, 14-15
Sacred sciences, 1
    Canon law as, 1
    Clergy required to study, 24
Schism, 50
Second Vatican Council, 31-32
Seminaries, 21-22

Social justice, obligation to
    promote, 18
SSPX, 7-8
St. Joseph Foundation, 16

Ukrainian Catholicism, 13-14

Valid, definition of, 7
Viaticum (see Eucharist)
Vocations, promotion of, 21